A TEXTBOOK O
LAPAROSCOPY FOR POSTGRADUATES

# THROUGH THE PORTS

## DR. S. R. DHAMOTHARAN

INDIA · SINGAPORE · MALAYSIA

# Notion Press

Old No. 38, New No. 6
McNichols Road, Chetpet
Chennai - 600 031

First Published by Notion Press 2019
Copyright © S. R. Dhamotharan 2019
All Rights Reserved.

ISBN 978-1-64546-550-8

# Contents

# Foreword

I am delighted that Professor S. R. Dhamotharan has chosen to crystallise his knowledge, thoughts & insights relating to Laparoscopic Surgery in this beautifully illustrated Textbook being brought out on the eve of his retirement from Government service.

The book is a practical guide to the management of major abdominal disease/condition through the laparoscopic approach. Explained in simple easy to understand format, illustrations in every chapter with valid brief pointers would be an immensely useful book for surgical trainees.

Over the past three decades, Laparoscopic surgery has revolutionized the practice of art and science of surgery, translating to significant benefit to patients. I am confident that this noble endeavor would undoubtedly empower the readership at large. Whilst expressing my heartfelt congratulations to a passionate teacher in Professor Dhamotharan, I sincerely wish & pray that he continues to devote much time to teaching and training even after his formal retirement.

**– Dr. P. Raghu Ram**

*MS, FRCS (Edin), FRCS (Eng), FRCS (Glasg), FRCS (Irel), FACS*
**Padma Shri awardee (2015)**

**DR.A.EDWIN JOE,M.D.,B.L.,**

DIRECTOR OF MEDICAL EDUCATION

**Address:**
162,EVR Periyar Salai, P.H,Road,
Kilpauk,Chennai-600 010.
**Contact No:**
Office : 044-28364501,502
Fax    : 044-28364500

## MESSAGE

I consider it my privilege to be writing the foreword of this book, "Textbook of Laparoscopy for Postgraduates" written by my good friend Professor Dr.Dhamotharan. Having known him personally for the past two decades, and having seen him in various capacities in many Govt. Medical Colleges of Tamilnadu, it's only apt that this book, primarily meant for postgraduates and passed out surgeons is written by him. Many around Dr.Dhamotharan agree that his zeal for teaching both undergraduates and postgraduates is unparalleled. It is safe to say that he is one of the last few of the old school of surgeons who actually "teach" the clinical concepts to the students. Having said this and having gone through the book, I consider it excellent since there is not a book like this for postgraduates which teaches them everything about laparoscopy in a way that will be understood and incorporated. Many of the diagrams given are hand drawn, and most of the concepts are explained in a simple way using the author's own words. I wish the author good luck for all his endeavours and everyone reading this book to have a great time.

**Dr.A.EDWIN JOE**
**DIRECTOR OF MEDICAL EDUATION**

This booklet written by Prof. Dr. S. R. Dhamotharan MS., FIAGES is a unique and pioneering work. The author has a long curve of teaching experience in Minimal Access Surgery. Though there are many books on laparoscopic surgery, this condensed booklet detailing the basic steps & procedures which are commonly done by any laparoscopic surgeon will be a ready reckoner. I could appreciate the involvement and the commitment of the author which is very much evident while going through the topics on Basic Laparoscopy.

The topics with illustrations makes anyone who does the surgery do it with ease and this book will be a useful addition to the shelves of Medical Libraries.

I wish the author all success!!

**– Prof. Dr. D. Maruthu Pandian MS., FAIS., FICS**

Former Dean and HOD of General Surgery
Govt Rajaji Hospital and Madurai Medical College
Chairman,
TN&P Chapter of ASI
Member,
Governing Council of NAtional ASI

# Preface

"UPDATE YOUR KNOWLEDGE IN THE FIELD OF MEDICINE
OTHERWISE YOU WILL BE OUTDATED"

These were the golden words that my Guru, Capt. Dr. V. Sathyavan told me when I was a post-graduate in General Surgery. This holds true to this day and will always be the mantra to success in accordance to "Survival Of the Fittest" in this ever – evolving field of surgery.

Minimal Access Surgery is a fast developing speciality which has a good future for General Surgery Post Graduates. For this very reason they must now acquire these new skills with laparoscopic surgery included as an integral part of the curriculum.

This book has been written to serve as a guide for beginners especially the post-graduates who wish to develop their skills in laparoscopy. It is hoped that this book will provide a solid foundation for their further training in the future!!

**– Prof. Dr. S. R. Dhamotharan MS., FIAGES**

Professor and HOD of General Surgery
Govt Rajaji Hospital & Madurai Medical College
Madurai.

# Acknowledgements

I take this opportunity to thank the Almighty, without whom this entire work is impossible.

I thank my wife Dr. Amba Bhavani MD and my daughter Dr. Abi Sindhuja MS General Surgery Post Graduate for their constant support and encouragement all through my career and especially during the course of the writing and publishing of this book. They had to make numerous sacrifices for me and till date they have never failed to support me.

I thank my teachers for inspiring me and making me what i am.

I thank all my colleagues for their support and valuable suggestions.

I wish to express my appreciation to the following Senior residents and Post graduates for their technical assistance in preparing this book.

Dr. Jaideep. P and Dr. Joel Danie Matthew – Senior Residents

Dr. Christeena Indrani and Dr. Vijayakumar. A – Senior Residents

Dr. Dorian Hanniel Terrence. S and Dr. Goutham. P – Postgraduates.

I would like to thank Notion Press, Chennai for their timely assistance in publishing my work into a beautiful product into your hands.

**– Prof. Dr. S. R. Dhamotharan MS., FIAGES,**

Professor and HOD of Surgery,
Govt Rajaji Hospital,
Madurai – 625020.

# Introduction

History of Laparoscopy is a story of many researchers. As you are all aware, our pioneers have met with many difficulties. But, because of their persistence and strong will-power they could stand firm to resist all adversities.

LAPAROSCOPIC APPENDICECTOMY – DEKOK performed the first Laparoscopy Assisted Appendicectomy in 1977.

LAPAROSCOPIC CHOLECYSTECTOMY – MAURET and LYON (France) Performed the first case of Laparoscopic Cholecystectomy in 1987.

LAPAROSCOPIC HERNIOPLASTY – In 1982 GER reported the first Laparoscopic Inguinal Hernia Repair.

LAPAROSCOPIC SURGERIES IN INDIA – Prof. TEHEMTON E. UDWADIA from Mumbai, India performed the First Laproscopic Cholecystectomy in India. He presented this work at the TENTH WORLD CONGRESS OF DIGESTIVE SURGERIES held at New Delhi in 1990 for creating awareness and spreading Laparoscopy in India. Thus the credit goes to Prof. TEHEMTON E. UDWADIA, rightly known as FATHER OF INDIAN LAPAROSCOPY.

# 1

# Basics of Laparoscopy

Laparoscopic procedures are very complex and detailed and hence assessment of the operative field is achieved only through optical systems and instruments. It is therefore very essential for a surgeon to know about the basics of this amazing technique of surgery to excel in the same.

## Laparoscopic Hardware

Basic laparoscopic instruments include the following:

   i)   Endovision System (Image chain)

  ii)   Endospacer (Insufflator)

 iii)   Electrosurgery unit (Diathermy)

 iv)   Suction/Irrigation system

  v)   Hand Instruments

All of these except the hand instruments are placed in a "Laparoscopic Trolley System"

A)   Monitor

B)   Light Source

C)   Camera Processor

D)   Insufflator

E)   Suction/Irrigation

F)   Electrosurgery Unit

i) **Endovision System (Image chain)**

a) Telescope Light cable & Light source

b) Camera head

c) Camera control unit – Video Monitor

d) Documentation

e) Integration system

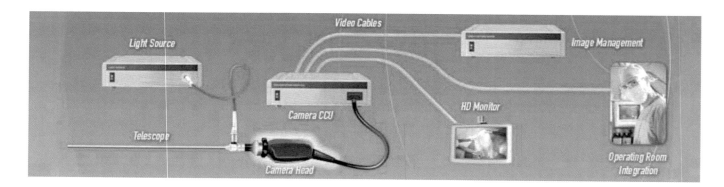

## Telescopes

They can be rigid or flexible telescopes. The ones which are commonly used are rigid ones like 0°, 30°, 45° with sizes 3 mm, 5 mm and 10 mm. The rigid scope works with the Hopkins Rod Lens System based on the principle of Total Internal Reflection.

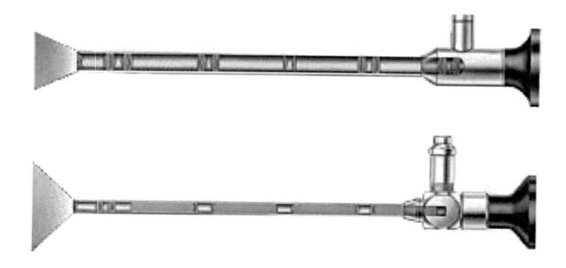

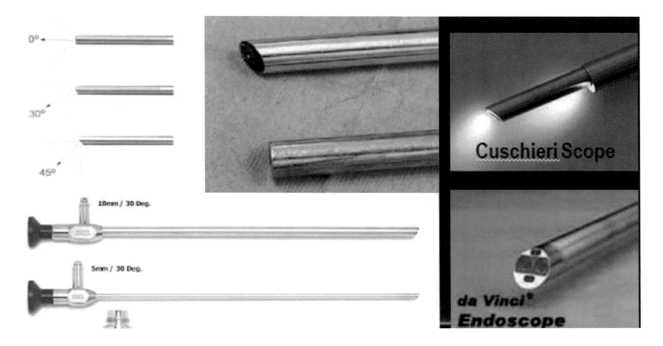

# Light cables

Two types of light cables are used. They are either Fibre optic cables or Liquid crystal gel cables. Any sharp bends or cracks in the plastic sheath warrants change of cable for good light transmission.

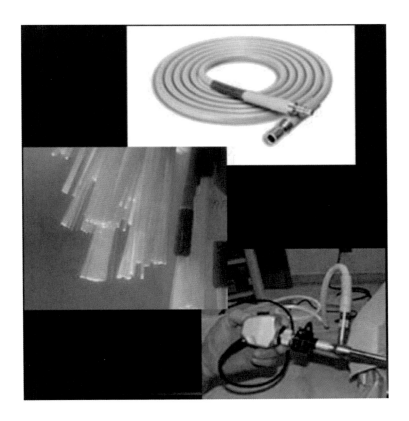

## Light source

"A good light source emits light as good as the sunlight"

Xenon/Halogen/Metal Halide lamps are used of which High intensity Xenon lamps provide better visual and photographic clarity.

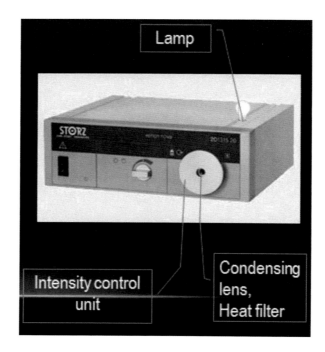

## Lamps

- Most important part of light source

- Quality of light depends on lamp used

- Quartz halogen

  ▶ Tungsten, efficient, low voltage, off white, hot, 2000 hrs life

- Xenon

  ▶ Cold, spherical/elliptical quartz, white, 1000 hrs life

  ▶ UV radiation (silica used for absorption)

- Metal halide vapor arc

  ▶ Mixture of rare earth salts, halides and mercury, white, 1000 hrs life

  ▶ Iron iodide, Gallium iodide

# Camera System

1.  Head of camera

    *   It is the "Eye of the surgeon"

    *   It has an Objective zoom lens and CCD (Charge Coupling Device)

    *   Resolution: average 250000 to 380000 pixels.

**CHARGED COUPLED DEVICE**

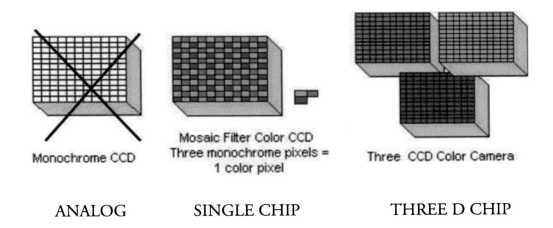

Monochrome CCD

Mosaic Filter Color CCD
Three monochrome pixels =
1 color pixel

Three CCD Color Camera

ANALOG          SINGLE CHIP          THREE D CHIP

2.  Camera Control Unit

    *   It is the "Brain of the endovision system"

    *   Has an Analog/Digital processor

3. Camera cable

Nowadays, even 3 D laparoscopic cameras are available.

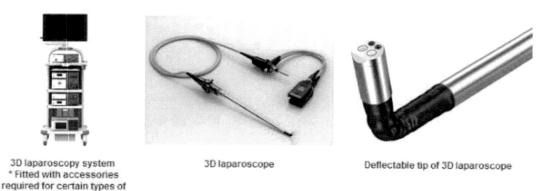

3D laparoscopy system
* Fitted with accessories
required for certain types of
examination

3D laparoscope

Deflectable tip of 3D laparoscope

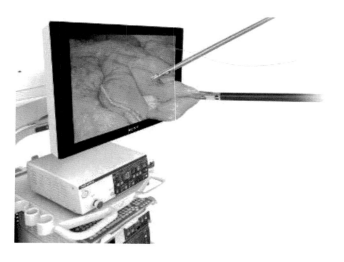

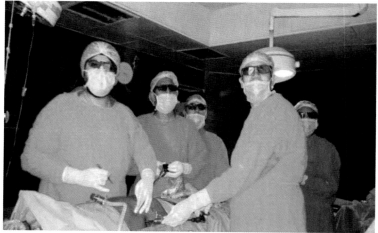

## Image Display

- Can use TV or Monitors

- CRT/LCD/LED DISPLAY

## Insufflator

The insufflator or Laparoflattor is used for controlled pressure insufflation of the peritoneal cavity to achieve adequate workspace required for the laparoscopic surgery. The pressure settings used are as follows:

- Adults 10–12 mm Hg

- Children 6–8 mm Hg

The flow rates are as follows:

- Veress 1 Lt/min

- Trocar 4 Lt/min

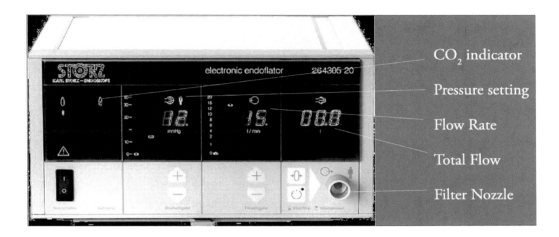

## Suction/Irrigation system

This is used for flushing the abdominal cavity and cleaning during endoscopic operative intrusions.

Irrigation system can also be used for HYDRODISSECTION.

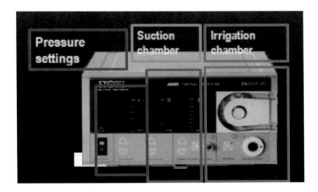

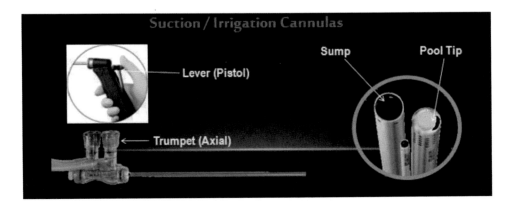

## Electrocautery

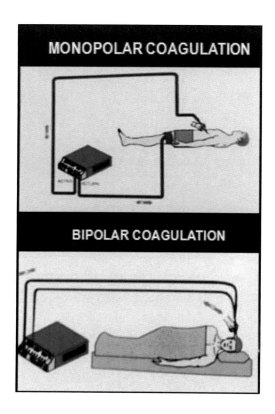

For Laparoscopic surgeries, 400 Watts diathermy should be used.

**Advantages of Monopolar Cautery:**

i) Ease of use.

ii) Instrument can be used for dissection also.

iii) Greater penetration of current density better hemostasis.

iv) Area of coagulation is twice that of bipolar cautery.

**Advantages of Bipolar Cautery:**

i) Less lateral thermal spread.

ii) Can be used in patients with pacemaker also, as it has less electrical interference.

iii) Power needed:

- Only 10% of monopolar.

- Output 50–100 ohms.

- Monopolar 30–300 ohms

# Harmonic Scalpel

Vessels are tamponaded and sealed by a protein coagulum.

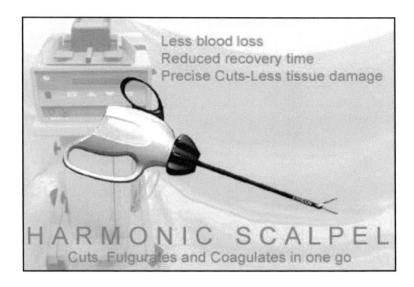

**Advantages:**

- Minimal lateral thermal injury.

- Less smoke production.

- It can be used to GRASP, DISSECT, CUT AND COAGULATE.

- No charring of tissues and thus clear planes of dissection can be achieved.

# Argon Plasma Coagulation

- It is a combination of Ionised argon gas and Monopolar cautery

- Bridges tissue and electrode and causes Denaturation of proteins causing Eschar formation.

**Disadvantages:**

a) Limited cutting ability.

b) Lack of tactile feedback.

c) Risk of Gas Embolism.

## Ligasure

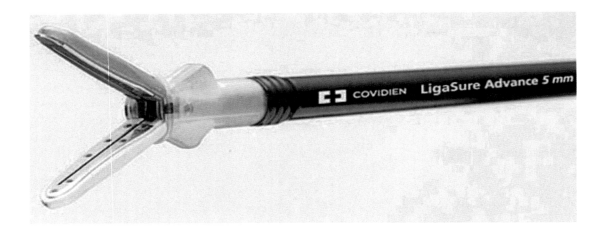

- Collagen and elastin within the tissue melt and reform to create the seal zone.

- Energy is pulsed and adaptive.

- Cycle is stopped when the response is complete.

- Uses high current (4 amps) and low voltage (<200 volts).

**Advantages:**

- Reduces thermal spread.

- No foreign body left behind.

- Upto 7 mm vessels can be coagulated.

- Burst pressure > 3 times the systolic BP.

- Takes only seconds to complete.

## Hand Instruments

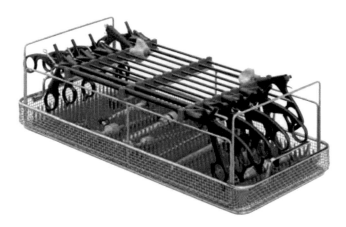

- Unlike Open Surgeries, Laparoscopic hand instruments are longer. The length varies from 37–50 cm.

- For bariatric surgeries, longer instruments and for paediatric surgery, smaller instruments are used.

- These are available in various sizes — 3/5/10 mm and can be used to grasp, dissect, shear, drive and suck.

- The various parts of the instrument include the jaw, inset, insulator and handle.

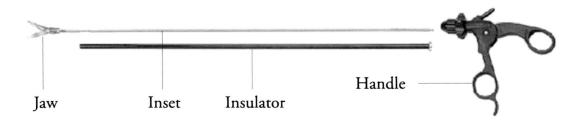

Jaw        Inset      Insulator        Handle

Depending upon the mechanism, various types of Handles are available namely pivot, axial, ball and pistol type

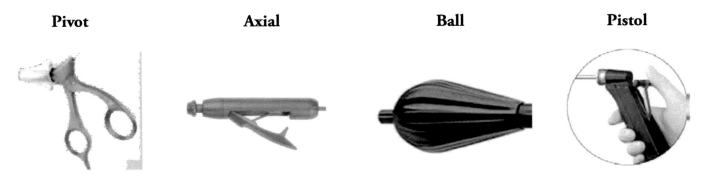

**Pivot**                    **Axial**                    **Ball**                    **Pistol**

**HANDLE PARTS:** A handle consists of

CAUTERY PIN

ROTATORY KNOB

RACHET

HOLDER

Handles can be racheted or non-racheted.

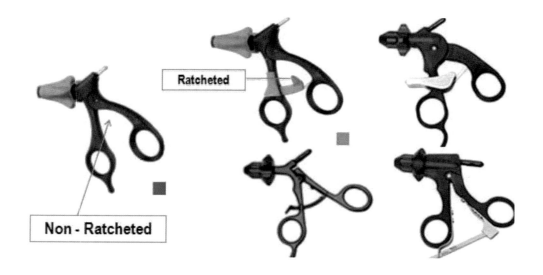

# Jaw Types

**SINGLE ACTION**

**DOUBLE ACTION**

**TRAUMATIC**

**ATRAUMATIC**

# Dissectors

Dissectors are of 4 types.

| CURVED (MARYLAND) | RIGHT ANGLED | STRAIGHT (DOLPHIN) | STRAIGHT (DUCKBILL) |

# Atraumatic Graspers

| FIXATION FORCEPS | BULLETNOSE GRASPER | BABCOCK | UNIVERSAL GRASPER |

# Scissors

| CURVED METZENBAUM | MICRO | HOOK | PERITONEAL |

# Technique of Gripping Instruments

Thumb is held outside the ring and the palm rests on the thumb ring. This is effective than finger in ring grasp. This significantly reduces the muscular forces used for catching hold of tissues.

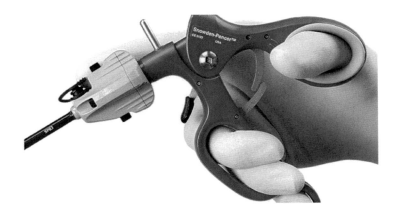

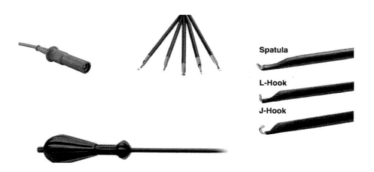

HIGH FREQUENCY ELECTRODES

## Veress Needle

Veress needle was first invented by a thoracic physician for the treatment and drainage of fluid in the pleura by taking advantage of the fact that it has a spring mechanism and blunt tip will not cause any injury of lung tissue. It has an an outer cannula and also a beveled needle point for cutting through tissues. The inner stylet consists of a spring which springs forward in response to the sudden decrease in pressure on crossing the abdominal wall and entering the abdominal cavity. It is used to create initial pneumoperitoneum to allow safe entry of trocars.

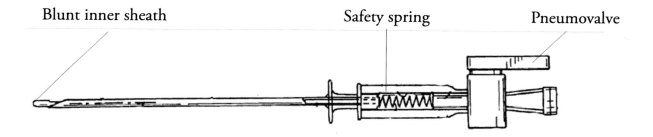

## Trocar

- Trocars pave a pathway for the laparoscopic hand instruments to access the peritoneal cavity.

- Trocars are available in different sizes and can be blunt or conical tipped and with or without blade.

- 5 mm and 10 mm trocars are available. Disposable and Reusable trocars are available.

- By using Visiport, camera port can be placed under vision.

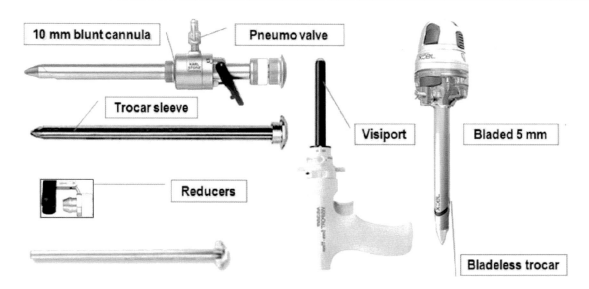

## Clip Applicator

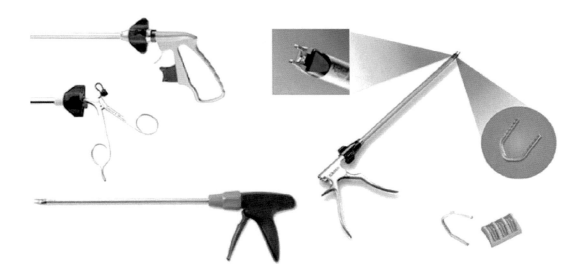

## Retractors

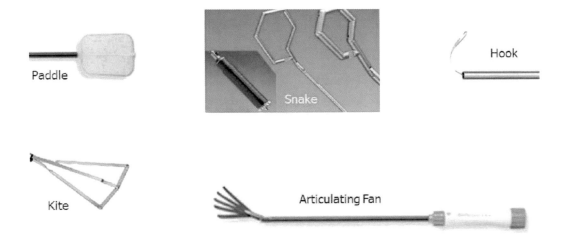

## Specimen Retreival Bags

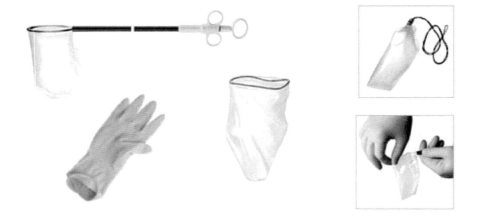

## Reducer

- Reducer is a device by which a 10 mm trocar is converted into 5 mm

- Allows 5 mm instruments to pass through 10 mm trocar without gas leak

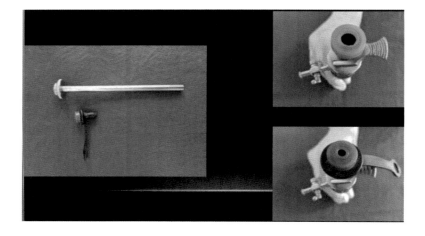

## Endo Loop Cannula

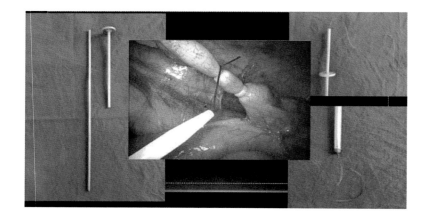

## Other Instruments

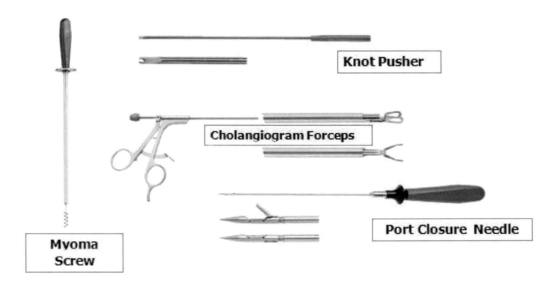

Knot Pusher

Cholangiogram Forceps

Port Closure Needle

Myoma Screw

## Creating Pneumoperitoneum

To ensure safe pneumoperitoneum generation, insert the needle

- In the midline.

- At an angle of 45° with the spine.

- Aimed towards the pelvis.

- With the patient in Trendelenberg position.

- Seizing and lifting the abdominal wall.

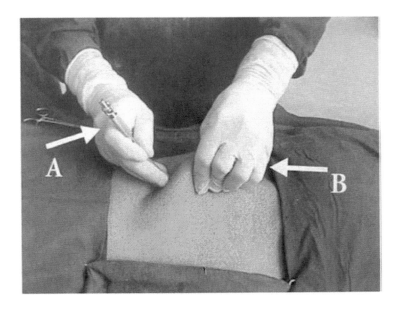

There are certain tests to be performed in sequence to confirm proper placement of the needle.

    i) **HISS TEST** – The air rushes into the negative pressure of the abdomen will create a classical Hissing sound.

    ii) **ASPIRATION TEST** – There is negative pressure in the abdomen and hence fluid inside the needle will flow into the abdomen and hence cannot be sucked back with a syring.

    iii) **NEGATIVE PRESSURE TEST** – Accentuation of negative pressure by elevation of the abdominal wall.

    iv) **EARLY INSUFFLATION PRESSURE** – Initially high pressure upto > 15 mmHg with low or no flow of gas means the needle's tip is incorrect In position.

    v) **VOLUME TEST** – If the static pressure as measured by the insufflator reaches 8–10 mmHg with less than 1 ltr of gas, it indicates incorrect placement.

Always remember!!! Umbilicus is at L4 level and 10% Aortic Bifurcation is below L4. Bifurcation can be as close as 1–2 cms. Hence entry into the abdomen with Veress needle must always be done with caution.

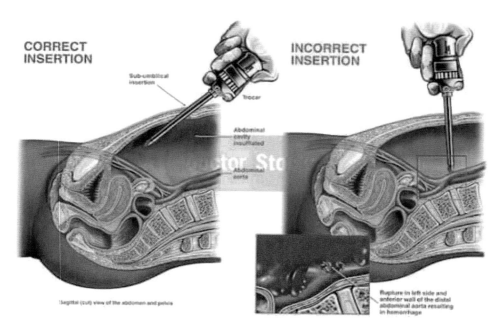

## Gas Insufflation

An ideal insufflating agent must be colourless, physiologically inert, non-explosive. It must have low tissue solubility and high blood solubility. It must also be readily available, inexpensive and non-toxic. The insufflating agents include $CO_2$, Nitrous oxide, helium and argon.

$CO_2$ is most commonly used as it is readily available, does not support combustion and has relatively low risk of venous gas embolism.

## Golden Rule of Gas Insufflation through Veress Needle

- Pressure < 5 mmHg

- Flow rate > 0.5 ltrs/min

## Ergonomics

Ergonomics is the applied science of equipment design, as for the workplace, intended to maximize productivity by reducing operator fatigue and discomfort.

## Port Placement

Port placement is the most important aspect of laparoscopic surgery and has been ever-evolving. It depends on various factors considering the patient's general condition, past surgical history, etc. An ideal port placement must have the following:

a)  Manipulation angle of 60°

b)  Equal Azimuth angle

c)  Elevation angle of 60°

d)  Intra: Extracorporeal shaft ratio of 2:1.

## Visual Display

Visualization of the surgical field differs in open and laproscopic surgeries. In open surgeries, the field of work = the visualization field. In laparoscopic surgeries, this differs.

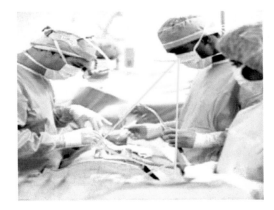 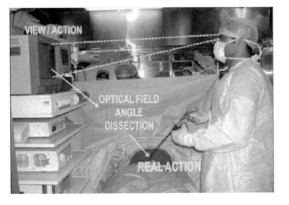

## Ideal Set-Up

- The surgeon, target and monitor must be in a co-axial line.

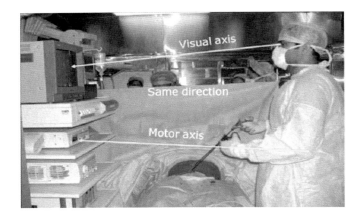

This leads to the visual and motor axis being in the same direction.

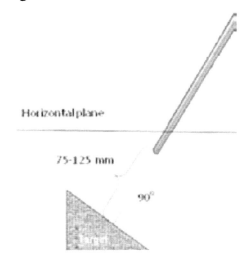

## Target View Planes

The Target to Endoscope distance should be 75–125 mm.

The Optic axis to Target view angle should be 90°

## Azimuth Angle

Azimuth angle is the angle between one instrument and the optical axis of the endoscope. The azimuth angles should always be equal. It should be 30–45* on each sides. Though achieving equal azimuth angles is not possible in many practical situation, better results are reported with equal azimuth angles.

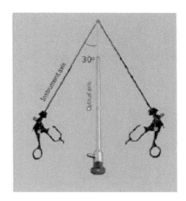

## Manipulation Angle

It is the angle between two working ports. The manipulation angle should be between 45–75°.

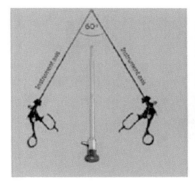

## Elevation Angle

It is the angle between the instrument and the horizontal plane. There exists a direct correlation between manipulation angle and elevation angle. So, ideal elevation angle is 45–75°.

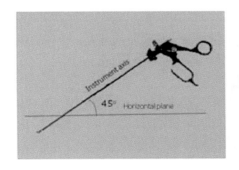

## Instrument Ratio

The intra-extra corporeal instrument ratio should be equal to or greater than 1.

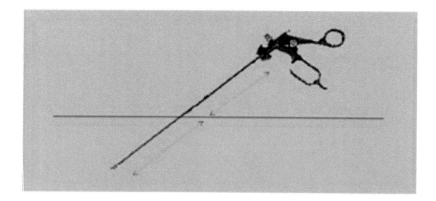

## Triangulation

To facilitate smooth manipulation and adequate visualisation, ports are placed in a triangular fashion. Here target is placed 15–20 cm from the centre port, and the two remaining ports are placed 5–7 cm from the centre port.

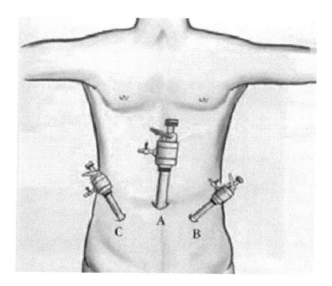

## Rule of Hand

For good ergonomics and for good manipulation and for good outcome of laparoscopic surgeries, one has to follow the rule of hand.

The distance between the camera port and the target organ should be the span of one hand. Working ports should be on either side of the camera port with six fingers breadth and the manipulation angle should be maintained at 60 degrees.

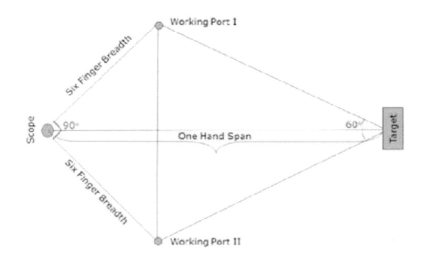

## EG: AN ILLUSTRATION FOR LAPAROSCOPIC CHOLECYSTECTOMY

TARGET - GB

OPTICAL PORT SITE

WORKING PORTS

WORKING PORT

WORKING PORTS

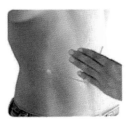

WORKING PORTS

TRIANGULATED PORTS

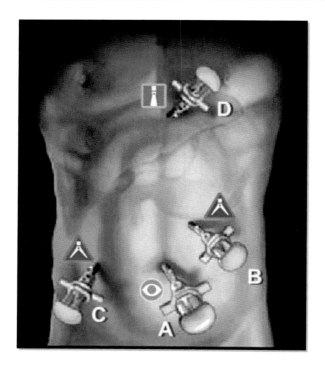

**French Position**

## Table Height

Table height must be at the appropriate level. In most laparoscopic surgeries it cannot be accomplished by lowering the operating tables alone as to compensate for various positions of the patient and heights of instruments. This limitation can be overcome by use of footboards by surgeons.

The height should be around 77 cm.

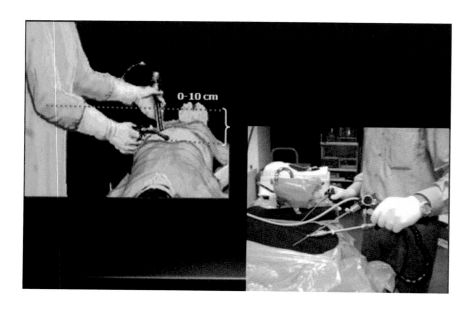

# Patient Positioning

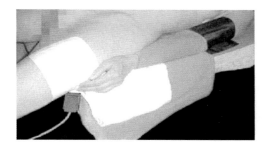 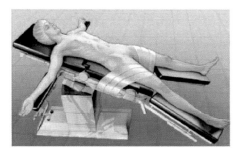

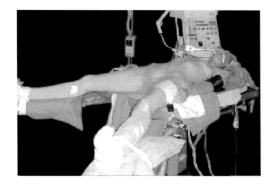 

In general patient must be placed in supine position with arms extended or tucked by the side or in various positions according to the procedure planned.

# Surgeon's Posture

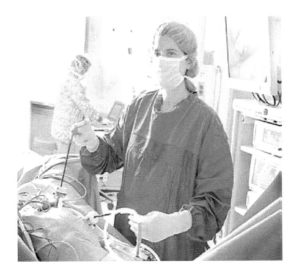

Surgeon must stand in a position that helps him/her hold the trunk very still. More frequent head movement is advisable during surgery with both the shoulders in relaxed position.

The angle of the elbows should be 90 degrees and > 120 degrees as shown in the picture.

## Team Location

Surgeon must stand in line with the target organ whereas cameraman must stand behind or to the side of the surgeon. The second assistant and nurse occupies the opposite side.

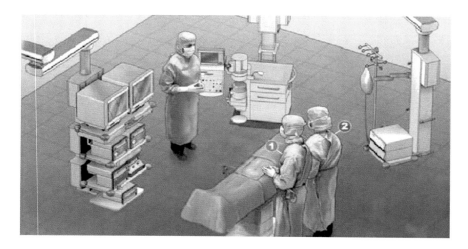

**CHALLENGES IN LAPAROSCOPIC SURGERIES**

## Depth Perception

Depth perception is usually meagre when compared to open surgeries. It usually prolongs the time taken for surgery and sometimes leads to injury of the organs which is overcome by continuous practice. Now, with the usage of 3D camera systems depth perception can be increased greatly.

## Tactile Feedback

Tactile feedback is usually accomplished by the muscles acting in thumb and forearm in response to the forces transmitted by them. It is less when compared to open surgeries. A laparoscopic surgeon must have good tactile feedback.

## Motion

Straight and stiff laparoscopic instruments offers limited degrees of motion. This forms an important pitfall.

## Camera Alignment

This is mainly contributed by poor ergonomics of the surgeon. Inexperienced or bored camera assistant moves the camera frequently and alters the horizon.

## Dexterity

Dexterity means the ability to use both hands skillfully and gracefully. In open surgeries, the right hand is the dominant one usually. But in laparoscopic surgeries, both hands must be used. It takes long time for the surgeons to get trained in laparoscopic procedures as it involves the maximum dexterity.

## Multiquadrant

Placement of ports is based on the various quadrants in which the surgery is going to be performed. This requires sound knowledge about the multiple quadrants in operating field.

## Surgical Scars

Presence of previous surgical scars makes the laparoscopic surgeries difficult.

## Magnification

Usual laparoscopy gives magnification of about 20 times than that of open surgeries. It is a double edged sword as it disturbs assessment of depth leading to injuries of organ

## Field of Vision

Laparoscopic surgeries always provides restricted field of vision with minimal lateral point of view. This interferes with our on table decisions based on injuries happening in the surrounding organs.

The acceptance of Minimal Access Surgery by the patient has made it mandatory for each surgical speciality to accept MAS as a part of their surgical skills. Surgeons have undergone a transition from a 3-dimensional visual and tactile environment, to a 2-dimensional visual and reduced tactile sensation format. The newer MAS techniques require longer learning curves and facility for more repetitive skills practice. It is hence mandatory for all general surgeons to know the basics of this modality.

# 2

# Pneumoperitoneum and Access to the Abdomen

Creation of pneumoperitoneum brings out a panoramic view of the entire abdomen, thereby facilitating space for our surgical dissection, suturing etc

- Two techniques for creation of pneumoperitoneum are:

    1. Closed technique

    2. Open technique

CLOSED TECHNIQUE:- Employs Veress needle to create pneumoperitoneum.

OPEN TECHNIQUE:- Employs Hasson cannula to create pneumoperitoneum.

## Access to Abdomen

Equipments required for acquiring access into the abdomen include:

- **Insufflator:-**

    The following parameters should be checked before starting the procedure:

    1. Flow rate (L/mt)

    2. Intraabdominal pressure (mm of Hg)

    3. Volume of gas insufflated (litres)

    4. $CO_2$ cylinder (check daily, keep a standby cylinder)

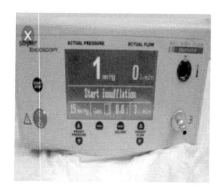

Testing the insufflators should be done when

i) The insufflation tube is not connected to needle

ii) Flow rate is 6 L/mt

iii) Pressure is 0 mm of Hg.

Pressure/flow shut off should be suspected during these conditions:

1. Flow rate < 1L/mt

2. Kinking of the tube

3. Increase in pressure > 30 mm Hg

## Gas Insufflation

**IDEAL INSUFFLATING AGENT** has the following properties:

a) Colorless

b) Physiologically inert

c) Non explosive

d) Low tissue solubility & high blood solubility

e) Readily available, inexpensive and nontoxic

**INSUFFLATING AGENTS** that are used are:

a) $CO_2$

b) Nitrous oxide

c) Helium

d) Argon

## Veress Needle

GOLDEN RULE OF GAS INSUFFLATION THROUGH VERESS NEEDLE

**Pressure <5 mmHg**        **Rate >0.5 ltrs/min**

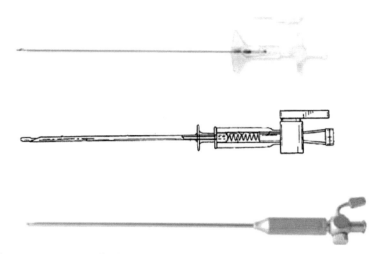

Things to be checked in Veress needle before procedure:

1. Patency of Veress needle by flushing saline through it.

2. Check for leaks by occluding the tip and push fluid under moderate pressure.

3. Push the blunt tip against the solid, flat surface – blunt tip should retract easily.

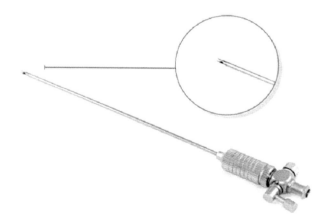

Testing the Veress needle:

- Low flow rate – 1 L/mt

- High flow – 2–2.5 L/mt

- Connected – Pressure should be < 3 mmHg

  – Pressure > 3 mmHg indicates blockage in

  1. Tube

  2. Hub

  3. Shaft

Maximal flow rate through Veress needle is 2.5 L/mt and through Hasson cannula is > 6 L/mt.

## Creation of Pneumoperitoneum

The site of insertion must be chosen. The optimal site is deep in the umbilicus, because

1. The abdominal wall is thinnest in that position and is made up of skin, fascia and peritoneum with no intervening fat.

2. The peritoneum is closely applied to the overlying fascia and does not peel off as it does in other sites. This decreases the possibility of extraperitoneal gas insufflations.

3. The incision is cosmetic and is often invisible within 2 to 3 weeks. To ensure safe pneumoperitoneum generation, insert the needle

   - In the midline.

   - At an angle of 45° with the spine.

   - Aimed towards the pelvis.

   - With the patient in Trendelenberg position.

   - Seizing and lifting the abdominal wall.

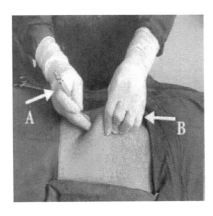 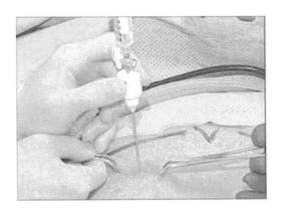 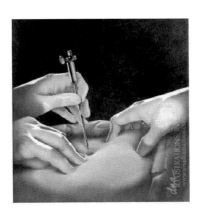

Hear the DOUBLE POP!

While inserting the veress needle, there will be initial resistance followed by a give-way while traversing the fascia and a second resistance while traversing the peritoneum.

## BEWARE OF CHANGES IN THE ANTERIOR ABDOMINAL WALL WITH WEIGHT

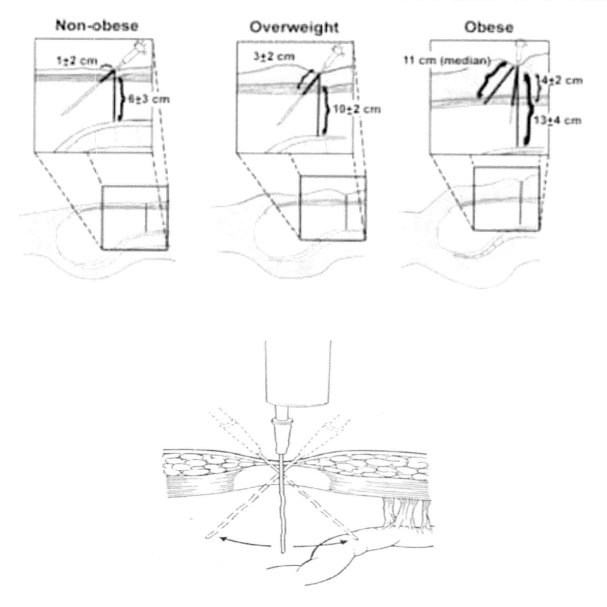

5 tests to be performed in sequence to confirm proper placement of needle:-

1. Hiss test:- Sound of air flowing into the negative pressure of the peritoneum

2. Aspiration test:- Fluid instilled into the peritoneal cavity will flow away from the needle and cannot be aspirated back.

3. Negative pressure test:- Accentuation of negative pressure by elevation of abdominal wall.

4. Early insufflation pressures:- Pressure of > 15 mmHg with low or no flow of gas indicate incorrect needle tip position.

5. Volume test:- If the static pressure as measured by the insufflator reaches 8–10 mm Hg with less than 1 ltr of gas, indicates incorrect placement.

# Trocars

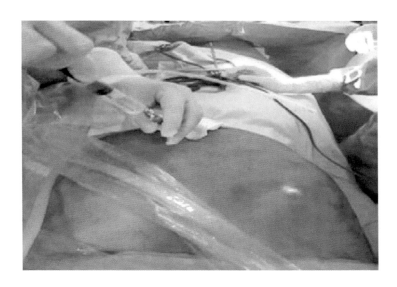

• Wide varieties of trocars are available.

• Both disposable and reusable are available.

TYPES:

• Sharp tip-tapered conical

• Pyramidal faceted

• Sharp trocar with safety shield

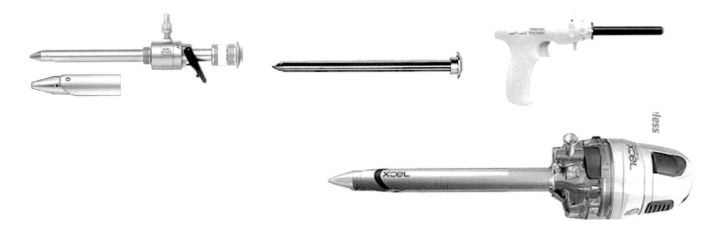

## Trocar Insertion:-

1. Always inspect the trocar and ensure all valves move smoothly.

2. Valve should be closed.

3. Safety shield should work properly.

4. Aim the trocar to pelvis.

5. There should be moderate resistance as the trocar is inserted.

6. Use twisting movement to introduce

7. Open the stopcock to confirm intraperitoneal placement

8. Subsequent trocar under direct vision.

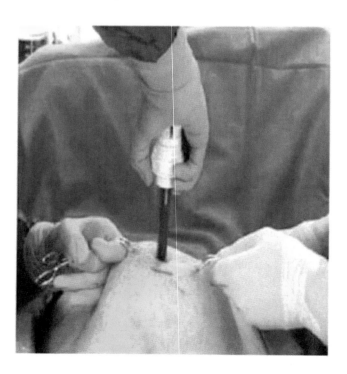 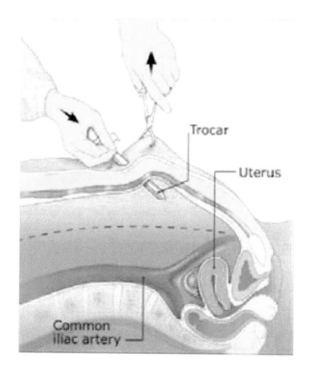

## Insertion of laparoscope, Secondary Trocars and Cannula

- After insertion of trocar, choice of laparoscope depends upon the purpose.

- A 5 mm telescope maybe inserted through the umbilicus without leaving any scar and may be satisfactory for simple examination of pelvis.

- If video is used or any laparoscopic surgery is to be performed, larger telescope is to be used.

- The place of insertion of secondary trocars are

  i) The midline about 4 cm above pubic symphysis

  ii) Within the safety triangle formed by umbilicus at its apex, the two obliterated umbilical arteries laterally and the pubic symphysis at its base. Instruments inserted within this area rarely damages inferior epigastric arteries

  iii) The secondary portal may be inserted lateral to the rectus abdominis on either side.

## Alternate Entry Sites

- UPPER ABDOMEN:- epigastrium, right hypochondrium, left hypochondrium

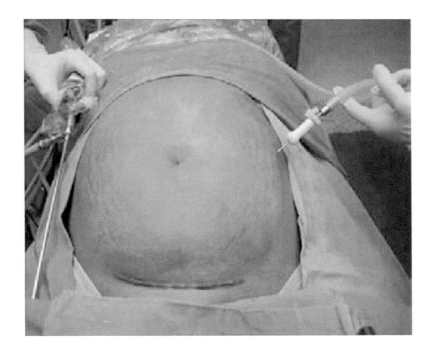

  o Prefer subcostal region

  o Percuss before needling

  o Decompress the stomach

- LOWER ABDOMEN:- right lower quadrant near MCBURNEY'S POINT

- Always decompress the bladder when using this quadrant.

- NINTH OR TENTH INTERCOSTAL SPACE

- TRANSUTERINE VERESS INSUFFLATION

## Open Technique of Creating Pneumoperitoneum

HASSON CANNULA:

- Hasson cannula is a cone shaped sleeve with metal or plastic sheath with a trumpet or flap valve and a Blunt tipped obturator.

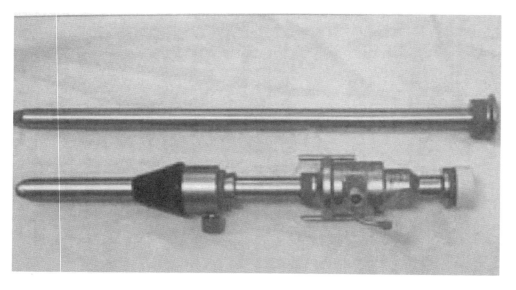

## Open Technique

- 2–3 cm transverse incision

- Dissect the subcutaneous tissue and fascia

- Identify the peritoneum, lift it with two hemostats and open sharply

   - Insert open cannula, fix the cannula with fascial Stitches.

- Saline gauze can be used to prevent leak

- It is a safe technique, can be performed by novice.

- Reduced risk of major complications as compared to closed technique, especially in relation to vascular injuries.

## Complications

- Bleeding from anterior abdominal wall

- Visceral injury

- Major vascular injury

# Management of Bowel Injuries

- Inspect the area of bowel injury when it is first introduced

- If the hole in bowel is of simple puncture-antibiotics and post op observation is enough

- Tangential laceration requires immediate suture either laparoscopically or by open laparotomy

- Laparoscopic resection and anastomosis

- Minilaparotomy

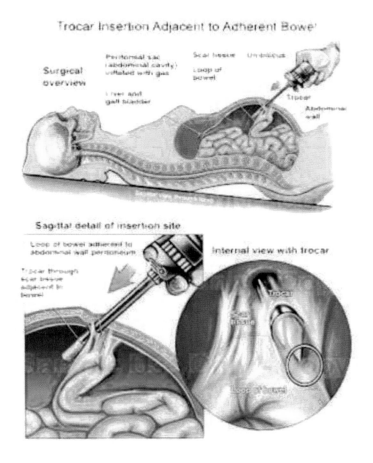

# Major Vascular Injuries

- It is usually due to sharp tip of Veress needle. If there is blood on aspiration, the needle should be removed and the abdomen repunctured.

- The retroperitoneum is fully examined to look for haematoma.

- In case of Central or expanding retroperitoneal hematoma, – laparotomy with retroperitoneal exploration is mandatory.

- In case of Hematomas in the mesentry and those located in lateral retroperitoneum – may be observed.

CORRECT INSERTION

Sub-umbilical insertion

Trocar

Abdominal cavity insufflated

Abdominal aorta

Sagittal (cut) view of the abdomen and pelvis

INCORRECT INSERTION

Rupture in left side and anterior wall of the distal abdominal aorta resulting in hemorrhage

## Complications

### I) BLEEDING FROM ABDOMINAL WALL

- It usually manifests as continuous stream of blood dripping from one of the trocars.

- Source of bleeding is usually inferior epigastric artery.

- It is controlled by variety of techniques include

  a) Application of direct pressure with port,

  b) Open or laparoscopic suture ligation or tamponade with a Foley's catheter.

## Recognition and Management

Suture must be in such a way that it enters abdomen on one side of trocar and exit on another side thereby encircling the full thickness of the abdominal wall.

## Optical Trocar

This is a technique which allows direct visualisation of each layer of abdomen with a 0-degree laparoscope as it is being traversed.

## Procedure

The optical trocar or port system is placed in to the incision with the 0 degree telescope perpendicular to the abdominal wall and it allows visualization by gently applying pressure on the abdomen while traversing.

When the peritoneum is breached and the omentum is visualized, camera is removed and the trocar withdrawn slightly and then cannula is advanced for 1–2 cm. After removal of the trocar, the scope is reintroduced. The omentum is visualized, which indicates correct placement of device.

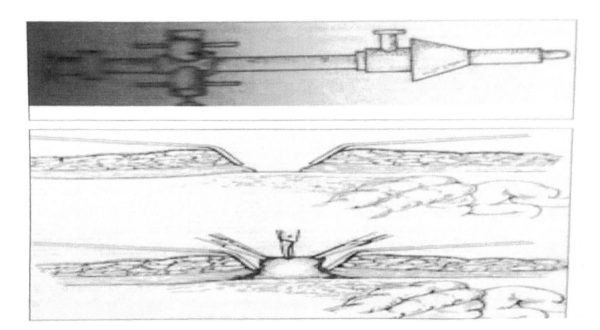

# 3

# Diagnostic Laparoscopy

Diagnostic laparoscopy plays an important role in the diagnosis and treatment of a number of surgical conditions.

## Technique

The surgeon must ensure normal functioning of the insufflator along with adequate supply of gas and that the electric generator, light source and video equipment are all in perfect order before starting the procedure.

## Anaesthesia

A general anaesthetic with muscle relaxation, endotracheal intubation and assisted respiration should be administered. Relaxation of abdominal muscles greatly facilitates the introduction and manipulation of instruments.

## Positioning of the Patient

Diagnostic laparoscopy requires a 15° Trendelenburg tilt. Lateral tilting helps to expose the pelvic side walls and is significant with respect to surgeries on kidneys, ureters, spleen, gall bladder and pelvic organs.

The patient is placed in the supine position with the legs abducted and supported in a modified lithotomy position. A diagnostic laparoscopy may be performed with legs flexed to 45° but the legs should be almost flat during laparoscopic pelvic surgeries to allow full range of movements of instruments. Care must be taken to avoid contact of patient's body to any metal objects to avoid the risks of getting electrosurgical burns.

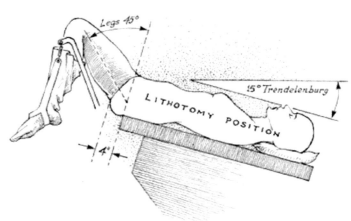

## Preparation

The abdominal wall should be cleansed with an antiseptic solution especially at the umbilicus. Bladder catheterisation and nasogastric tube insertion are also prerequisites.

## Insertion of Veress needle

Surgeon must ensure that the Veress needle is patent and its spring mechanism is working. It should be connected to the pneumosufflator and gas turned on so that the basal pressure in the system can be noted. Insufflation pressure should not rise more than 5–10 mm Hg above this pressure.

Umbilicus is ideally preferred for entry. Alternative sites are selected if adhesions are suspected. Other possible sites commonly used are lateral to the umbilicus at the same level, suprapubically in the midline, Palmer's point, or posterior vaginal fornix.

The technique of needle insertion through the umbilicus is as follows:

1. A small incision is made in the depth of the umbilicus.

2. The abdominal wall is held up with the free hand to prevent damage to the underlying deep viscera and great vessels.

3. Veress needle is inserted at right angles to the surface and at 45° to the horizontal to prevent extraperitoneal insufflations of gas or injury to blood vessels.

4. The position of needle is then confirmed by aspiration test, either by injecting air or saline through a 20 ml syringe attached to the same.

5. Induction of pneumoperitoneum by insufflating $CO_2$ at 1L/min. Once it is established, the presence of sufficient intra-abdominal space into which the laparoscope can be introduced safely is confirmed by the Hiss and Aspiration test.

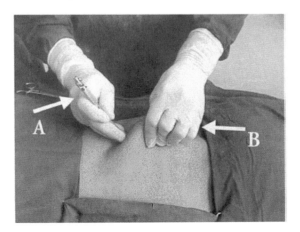

An alternative way for the induction of pneumoperitoneum is by the open (Hasson) method.

## Insertion of primary trocar and cannula

The primary trocar and cannula is inserted now. The trocar is held firmly with the flattened proximal end of the trocar in the heel of the hand. During insertion the upper abdominal wall should be compressed by the free hand to make the lower abdomen tense. The trocar must be advanced along a zig-zag pathway to prevent incisional hernia and the extended forefinger should act as a guard to prevent sudden uncontrolled insertion.

## Insertion of Laparoscope

A 10 mm telescope is preferred to a 5 mm one as the field of vision is enhanced.

When the trocar is inserted and gas heard to escape through the cannula which confirms the tip is in the peritoneal cavity, a warmed telescope to which a camera has been attached is introduced and advanced under direct vision into the peritoneal cavity.

## Insertion of Secondary Trocars and Cannulae

Sites of secondary ports include:

1. The midline about 4 cm above the pubic symphysis.

2. Within the 'safety triangle' formed by the umbilicus at its apex, the two obliterated umbilical arteries laterally and the pubic symphysis at its base. This would avoid damge to the inferior epigastric vessels.

3. Lateral to the rectus abdominis on either side. The instruments are always angled towards the pouch of Douglas with the uterus held in anteversion, under direct laparoscopic observation.

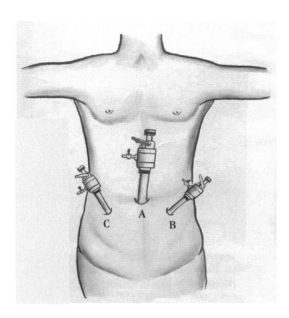

## Systematic Inspection of the Abdominal and Pelvic Organs

**Upper abdomen**

Systematic examination is carried out in the following order.

1. Caecum and appendix

2. Ascending colon till the hepatic flexure

3. Right lobe of liver and Gall bladder

4. Left lobe of liver, stomach and spleen

5. Descending colon

6. Sigmoid colon

It may be necessary to alter the Trendelenburg tilt to obtain a good view of the upper abdominal organs.

## Pelvic Organs

The organs examined systematically as follows:

1. Uterus

2. Anterior cul-de-sac

3. Right Fallopian tube

4. Right Ovary

5. Right broad ligament

6. Right uterosacral ligament and Pouch of Douglas

7. Left side of the pelvis in the reverse order.

## Skin Closure

Once the diagnostic survey has been completed, the ancillary instruments and their cannulae are removed and the puncture sites carefully examined. Gas is allowed to escape and the principal cannula is removed.

Abdominal incision is closed a non absorbable suture which is removed in 5–7 days. Alternatively, a subcutaneous absorbable suture may be used.

## Indications for Diagnostic Laparoscopy

These can be divided into Surgical and Gynaecological.

| General Surgery | Gynaecological |
|---|---|
| Staging of intra-abdominal malignancies | Pelvic Inflammatory Disease |
| Cryptorchidism | Infertility |
| Trauma | Endometriosis |
| Nonspecific abdominal pain | Ectopic pregnancy |
| | Uterine abnormalities |
| | Tubal pathologies |

Diagnostic laparoscopy is useful in the staging of many intra-abdominal malignancies like esophageal cancer, gastric cancer, pancreatic cancers, liver cancers, biliary cancers, colorectal cancers and lymphomas.

## Contraindications to Laparoscopy
### Absolute Contraindications

1. Irreducible external hernias

2. Hypovolemic shock

3. Coincidental medical conditions like Cardiorespiratory embarrassment, recent myocardial infarction etc

4. Lack of facilities

## Relative Contraindications

1. Generalised peritonitis

2. Intestinal obstruction or ileus

3. Obesity

4. Local skin infections.

# Principles of Operative Laparoscopy

## General Principles of Laparoscopic Surgery

The safe performance of laparoscopic surgery demands the meticulous observation of certain basic principles

1. There must always be a proper indication for laparoscopic surgery.

2. General anesthesia with adequate muscle relaxation is a must.

3. Availability of instruments.

4. Adequate assisting staff

5. Adequate working space

6. Gentle tissue handling

7. Recognition of anatomical landmarks.

    a) Intra-abdominal structures

    b) Intra-pelvic structures

    c) Retroperitoneal structures

8. Care during electrocautery

9. Skill and expertise to continue with or to convert to open surgery when required.

## Specific Principles of Laparoscopic Surgery

### Position of Surgeon

A right handed surgeon should stand on patient's left. The laparoscope is inserted through umbilicus. It is always necessary to use closed circuit television and work while viewing the video screen. Usually, the surgeon holds the laparoscope and camera in his/her right hand. An assistant steadies the tissues with grasping forceps and the surgeon holds the active instrument in the left hand.

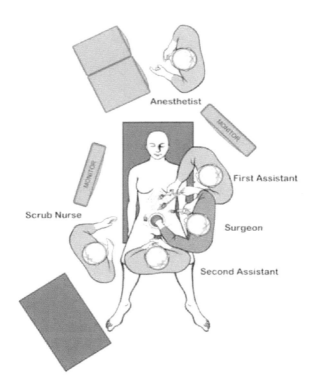

## Sites of Secondary Portals

Two secondary portals are usually needed through which ancillary instruments are introduced. The number of ports used is according to the surgeon's preference.

1. Most laparoscopic surgeries are practised through the 'safety triangle' which has its apex at umbilicus, base at pubic symphysis with lateral walls as the line of obliterated umbilical artery on either side. Incisions within this triangle avoids the deep inferior epigastric arteries.

2. The incisions should be far enough apart so that the instruments do not get in each others' way providing a reasonable divergent angle.

3. A more lateral incision is preferred in some cases.

4. Presence of multiple adhesions may dictate the choice of an alternative site.

5. The portals should be far enough from the target tissues to allow easy approach with scissors or forceps.

## Hemostasis

Bleeding is often less in laparoscopic surgery because:

a) The intra-abdominal pressure which is usually 15 mm Hg is higher than the venous pressure and hence bleeding from small vessels tends to stop quickly

b) Warm lavage solution has a hemostatic effect.

c) Better view of the target tissue helps in easy identification of vessels.

It is always preferable to ensure that blood vessels are occluded before dividing. Hemostasis may be achieved by coagulation using bipolar or monopolar current, thermal energy upto 120–140 ˚C or by ligation with sutures or clips along with injection of vasoconstrictive solutions.

## Ligatures

Ligatures may be applied to a pedicle with modified Roeder loop (endoloop) or by intra- or extra-corporeal knotting.

The **Roeder loop** consists of a plastic applicator with a snap-off end and a loop of suture material with a pre-tied slip knot. The ligature is inserted into the abdomen through an introducing channel which fits into a standard 5 mm cannula. The technique of application is as follows:

1. The loop and applicator are backloaded into the introducer. The applicator is advanced until the loop is completely within.

2. The introducer with endoloop is inserted into abdomen through 5 mm cannula and loop placed over pedicle.

3. A grasping forceps is inserted through a contralateral cannula.

4. Pedicle is grasped and drawn upwards through the loop.

5. Knot is pushed down onto the pedicle and ligature positioned on the pedicle by a combination of manipulating the grasper and tightening the endoloop.

6. The grasping forceps are removed and both hands are used to tighten the ligature.

7. Ligature is cut about 0.5 cm from the knot.

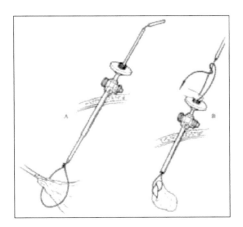
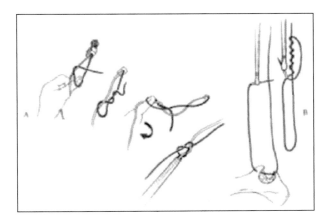

## Suturing Techniques

Sutures may be inserted laparoscopically and the knots tied outside the abdomen (extracorporeal knotting) or within (intra-corporeal knotting).

In **extracorporeal knotting,** the suture is passed through the tissue and then brought outside the abdomen through the cannula to tie the knot.

### Technique

1. The needle and suture are held in the needle holder and loaded into the introducer.

2. Introducer is inserted into abdomen through 5 mm cannula.

3. The needle holder grasps the needle and the needle angle is altered with the grasper until its perpendicular to the axis of the holder and grasper is disengaged.

4. Needle is passed through the tissue and passed back to needle holder and suture pulled through the tissue.

5. Needle is withdrawn and the suture ends are tied into a single knot outside the abdomen (extracorporeal).

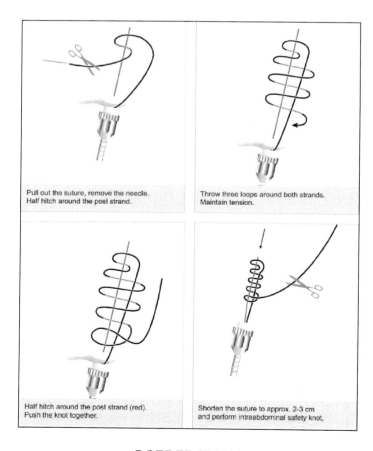

ROEDER KNOT

**Intracorporeal knotting** though technically difficult is a standard procedure.

**Technique**

1.  The needle holder is passed through the cannula and the suture is grasped at 15 cm from the needle.

2.  Cannula with the needle holder is reinserted carrying the suture.

3.  Grasping forceps are introduced and needle pulled into the peritoneal cavity.

4.  The needle is pushed through the tissue and held by the grasping forceps and the suture is pulled through the tissue until about 5 cm remains.

5.  The needle is then held in the grasper with its point in the same direction as the short end of the suture. A double loop is made and knot pulled tight to complete the surgical knot (intra-corporeal).

Nylon or PDS sutures are favoured.

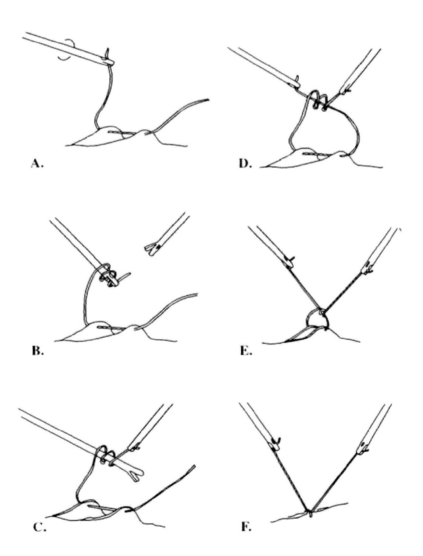

## Clips and Staples

Hemostatic clips are invaluable in situations where use of high frequency currents or thermocoagulation are technically difficult. Staples have enabled more advanced laparoscopic surgeries to be performed easily but are not suitable to occlude a bleeder.

## Vasoconstriction

Vasopressin at 5 IU in 100 ml of normal saline or Adrenaline in 1:200000 can be used as vasoconstrictors to secure hemostasis.

## Lasers

Carbon dioxide laser is most commonly used for laparoscopic surgery with excellent precise cutting properties but is not hemostatic. Nd:YAG laser is hemostatic but can produce tissue damages due to increased depth of penetration.

## Prevention of Adhesions

1. Gentle tissue handling.

2. Prevent desiccation.

3. Hemostasis.

4. Accurate approximation of tissues.

5. Appropriate choice of suture materials and proper knot placement.

6. Adjuvants like fibrin glue or heparinised salt solution.

## Adhesiolysis

Adhesiolysis should commence at the abdominal wall and caudally proceed towards the pouch of Douglas. It may be performed with scissors, monopolar microneedle or laser which should always approach the adhesion at right angles. Scissor dissection may be close to the organ but electric energy or laser must be applied 1–2 mm away from the organ to prevent lateral damage due to heat. Adhesions can be prevented by peritoneal lavage which removes blood, fibrin and debris.

## Hydrodissection

Hydrostatic pressure can be used to dissect the tissues. Sophisticated systems are attached to automated pumps allowing irrigation and suction. The tip of the cannula is placed behind the adhesion. When the fluid is turned on, it would find the path of least resistance atraumatically creating a line of dissection. The adhesion can now be divided. Hydrodissection may also be used to provide a fluid backstop for $CO_2$ laser.

Removal of instruments is always done under direct vision.

Closure of wounds is done with sutures or clips. Incisions more than 5 mm are to be closed in 2 layers to prevent hernia formation.

# 4

# Laparoscopic Appendicectomy

**History:**

In 1983, Kurt Semm, a gynaecologist from Germany did the first laparoscopic appendicectomy. In 1987, Schrieber reported laparoscopic appendicectomies in women.

## Advantage

In the following situations, laparoscopic appendicectomy scores over open appendicectomy. These are,

1. Vague chronic abdominal pain where diagnostic laparoscopy culminates in appendicectomy.

2. RIF pain in young women where there is confusion in diagnosis.

3. Abnormal positions of appendix such as subhepatic or situs inversus.

4. An accurate diagnosis can be made and the appendix can be removed at the same time.

5. Obese individuals where large incision is required.

6. In diabetics, who have a high chance of wound infection.

7. Interval appendicectomy, in which recovery is faster.

## Patients in Whom Caution Is Reqiured

1. Those who are poor risk of general anaesthesia.

2. Imaging shows formation of abdominal mass

3. Patients with previous abdominal surgery

4. Patients with stump appendicitis or burst appendix.

**Always consent is obtained for conversion to open appendicectomy.**

## Contraindications

It is relatively contraindicated in previous lower abdominal surgery, pregnancy with appendicitis, malignancy, palpable appendicular mass, immunosuppressed individual, comorbid status.

# Instruments

## Exposure and Manipulation

1. Veress needle

2. 10 mm port – 2

3. 5 mm port – 1

4. 30 degree camera with light source, monitor, $CO_2$ cylinder and insufflators

## Cutting and Coagulation

1. Maryland dissector

2. Babcock dissector

3. Bipolar forceps

4. Scissors

5. Suction irrigation

6. Endoloops ligatures

7. Endobag

## Preparation

1. Adequate hydration

2. Preoperative antibiotics

3. A nasogastric tube in the presence of ileus, generalized peritonitis or repeated vomiting

4. Foley's catheter to decompress the bladder.

# Anaesthesia-GA

## Positions

Patient is in supine position with a Trendelenburg tilt and when the surgeon is ready to proceed, the patient's right side is tilted up. In this position, the ascending colon is slightly suspended from the lateral wall and the small intestine falls away from the operative field.

Monitor is kept on right side

Surgeon stands on left side

Camera assistant will stand on the right of the surgeon or diagonally opposite the surgeon on the right side.

The scrub nurse will stand at the foot of the table at the right side.

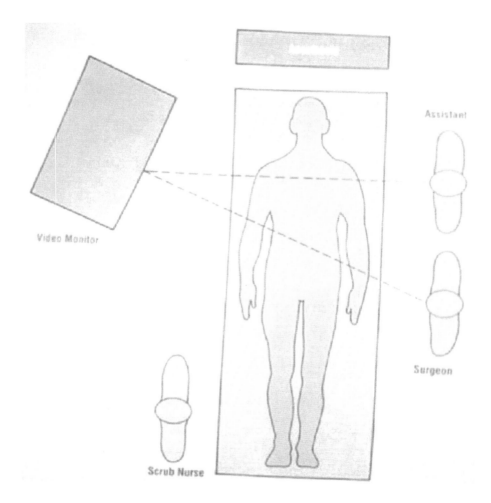

The appendix should be removed even if it is macroscopically normal for two reasons — 1) The patient has been admitted with a history suggestive of appendicictis and likely to present in the future with the same symptoms. 2) Even if the appendix looks externally normal, the histological report usually confirms the diagnosis of acute appendicitis.

Laparoscopic appendicectomy can be performed in two ways

1.  Intra-corporeal appendicectomy

2.  Laparoscopically assisted appendicectomy

## Intra-Corporeal Appendicectomy

- A 'smile' or vertical incision is made just below the umbilicus in midline.

- Pneumoperitoneum needle is inserted.

- Once the position of the needle is confirmed, insufflations of the abdomen is done.

- Insufflation is continued to a preset pressure of 14 mmHg.

- 10 mm trocar is introduced. A telescope with light cable and camera attached is inserted.

- Laparoscopic exploration of the abdomen is done.

- All the accessory trocars should be placed under direct vision. This eliminates the risk of damage to adjacent tissues.

## Standard Four Port Appendicectomy

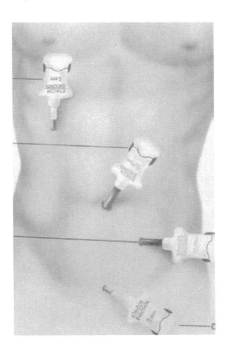

- Once the caecum is identified, the base of the appendix is identified by the confluence of the taenia.

- Introduce a 5 mm straight grasper through the port in the right upper quadrant.

- Grasp the caecum and pull it superiorly to expose the appendix.

- With a second grasper through the suprapubic port, grasp the mesoappendix and retract the grasper slightly, creating tension on the mesoappendix.

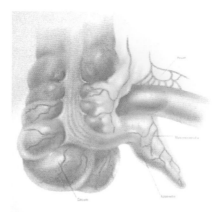

- An electrosurgery probe with hook dissector through the left lateral port.

- Cauterization of the mesoappendix is begun at the top of the mesoappendix.

- As dissection proceeds, the top of the appendix is grasped and pushed anteriorly to keep it out of the way of the dissection forceps.

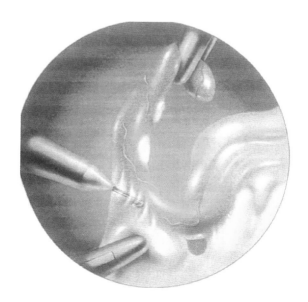

- In this way the whole of the mesentery is separated from the appendix.

- Then the base of the appendix is ligated by a endoloop suture.

- Technique of passing the endoloop ligature is as follows;

  - Endoloop ligature is a preknotted suture that can be inserted into the abdominal cavity and placed over a structure. A pusher rod advances the knot into place to insure effective ligation.

  - Back load the endoloop ligature into a 5 mm reducing sleeve.

  - Retract the loop so it is completely inside the reducing sleeve.

  - Under direct vision, advance the endoloop ligature until the loop is exposed inside the abdomen.

  - A 5 mm grasper is introduced through the suprapubic port and place the suture loop over the tip of the grasper.

  - With the grasper, lift the tip of the appendix, allowing the ligature to be manipulated into position — to the appendiceal cecal junction.

  - Once the ligature has been positioned and the knot closed, the knot should be tightened again. Then the tail of the ligature is cut.

  - Three endoloop ligatures are used.

  - First two are placed proximally.

  - Third one is placed distally, 6–7 mm above the distal most of other two ligatures. The tail of the third ligature is not cut.

The appendix is then divided between the proximal two loops and the distal loop with scissors introduced through the left iliac fossa.

- The appendix is detached through the left lateral port. Altrenatively an endobag can be used.

- Hemostasis is ensured.

- Saline irrigation is done.

- Choice of leaving a drain is dictated on a case basis.

- Instruments are removed from the abdomen.

- Incisions are sutured.

# Complications of Laparoscopic Appendicectomy

1. Injury to bowel, vessels while passing ports.

2. Complications of pneumoperitoneum.

3. Accidental cautery injury to bowel, vessels and other structures.

4. Bleeding, bowel perforation and peritonitis

5. Slipping of ligature, leak, peritonitis and fistula formation.

# Special Clinical Circumstances

- PREGNANCY:

  o Appendicitis occurs in equal frequency in pregnant and non-pregnant women and the natural history is unaffected by the stage of pregnancy.

  o When associated with perforation and peritonitis, there is significant maternal mortality and morbidity as well as fetal loss.

  o Access to the appendix can be hampered by the presence of an enlarged uterus.

  o Laparoscopic appendicectomy should be attempted in pregnant women by experienced, advanced laparoscopic surgeons.

  o Open access using the Hassan technique is a must.

  o The intra abdominal pressure should be kept at 10–12 mm Hg

- NECROSIS OF THE BASE OF THE APPENDIX:

  Necrosis of the base of the appendix with or without involvement of the caecal wall warrants limited caecal resection.

- CHRON'S DISEASE:

  Here, medical treatment is instituted and appendix is not removed to avoid appendiceal stump leakage or fistula.

# 5

# Laparoscopic Cholecystectomy

Gall stone occurence is one of the commonest diseases treated by surgeon.

One of the methods of laparoscopic cholecystectomy will be discussed below.

Any laparoscopic procedure demands surgeons eye, hand, operative field and monitor in one line. Some important anatomy related to laparoscopic cholecystectomy is discussed first.

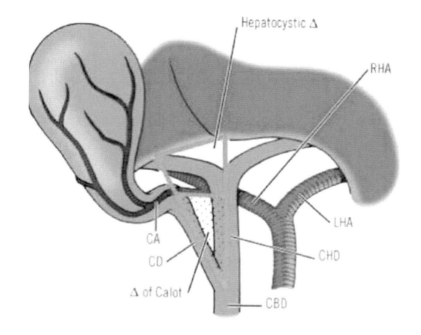

## Hepatocystic Triangle

Hepatocystic triangle is an important imaginary reference for laparoscopic cholecystectomy. It is bounded by common hepatic duct, cystic duct and inferior liver surface. The importance of this triangle is the cystic artery arises within this triangle. Calot's triangle is bounded by common hepatic duct, cystic duct and cystic artery and it is a component of hepatocystic triangle.

## Position

Equipment/monitor position is very important such that it is easily visualized by all surgical team members. Intra abdominal pressure and gas flow monitor should be in clear site to the surgeon. Patient placed supine with arms either wrapped at the sides or at right angles. Both legs are either wrapped or placed in elastic stockings to prevent Deep venous thrombosis due to decreased venous return caused by increased intra abdominal pressure from pneumoperitoneum.

## Laparoscopic Cholecystectomy Comprises of 4 Steps

STEP 1 – creation of pneumoperitoneum and insertion of trocar

STEP 2 – separation of all adhesions to gall bladder and surrounding liver with exposure of peritoneal fold in which the cystic duct and artery are situated.

STEP 3 – dissection and skeletonisation of cystic duct and cystic artery and occlusion and division of these structures.

STEP 4 – dissection and extraction of gall bladder and closure of incision.

## Usual trocar insertion are

1. 1 cm long infra umbilical incision for telescope.

2. 5 mm incision in right mid axillary line (5 to 8 cm below rib margin).

3. 5 mm incision in right midclavicular line 2 cm below costal margin.

4. 1 cm incision at the junction of upper one third and lower two third of line between xiphisternum and umbilicus.

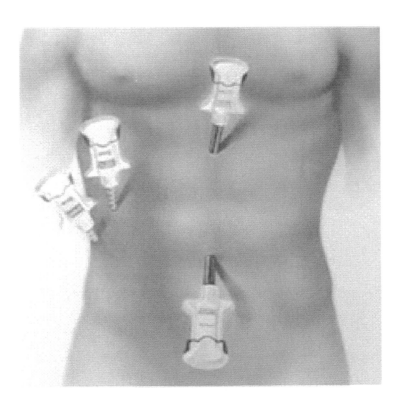

**STEP 1:**

**Creation of pneumoperitoneum and trocar entry as discussed earlier.**

**After** insertion of camera port quick inspection is done of peritoneal cavity to exclude other pathology and iatrogenic injury. It is important to note that all accessory trocars should be pointed in the direction of gall bladder as it is necessary to minimize trauma to abdominal wall by avoiding angulation of trocar towards gall bladder.

Then a 5 mm trocar is inserted in the right mid axillary line which is used to displace the fundus of gallbladder headwards and caecum and ascending colon identified to ensure the site of penetration is anterior to peritoneal reflection of these structures.

Then a 5 mm trocar is inserted in mid clavicular line. Instruments manipulated by surgeons left hand will pass through this trocar. Whereas instruments used in right hand will pass through epigastric port. Then epigastric trocar is inserted just right to falciform ligament

**STEP 2:**

After insertion of trocar and after visualization of peritoneum and other organs, all adhesions which impair visualization and retraction of gall bladder should be divided by unipolar or bipolar diathermy. Then with the help of grasping forceps, fundus of gall bladder retracted towards the right shoulder (as depicted in the image below) exposing the body and adhesions around the gall bladder. Adequate retraction of gall bladder is a prerequisite of laparoscopic cholecystectomy.

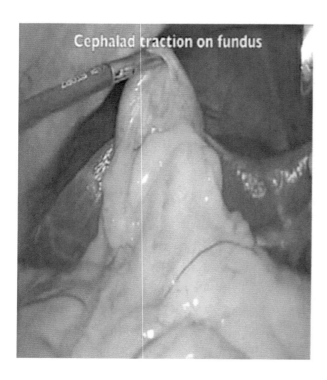
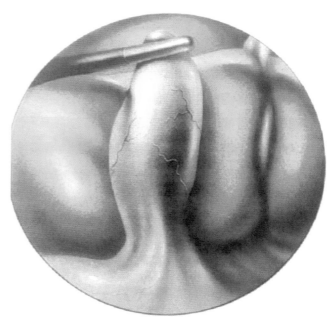

**Factors responsible for difficulty during retraction,**

A) Grossly distended Gall bladder

B) Contracted/fibrosed gall bladder which may require a 5<sup>th</sup> trocar in the left hypochondriacal region for direct liver retraction.

C) Very thick walled gall bladder which require toothed grasper for retraction.

D) A stone impacted in the neck of gall bladder

E) Anterior and superior surface of gall bladder adherent to anterior abdominal wall or diaphragm. Mostly these adhesions are avascular and so can be easily divided.

F) Fibrotic or cirrhotic liver in which a 5<sup>th</sup> port can be used for liver retraction.

The adhesions should be removed close to gall bladder as much as possible thus shearing them of the gall bladder in an avascular plane. Then all adhesions to liver adjacent to gall bladder to be removed.

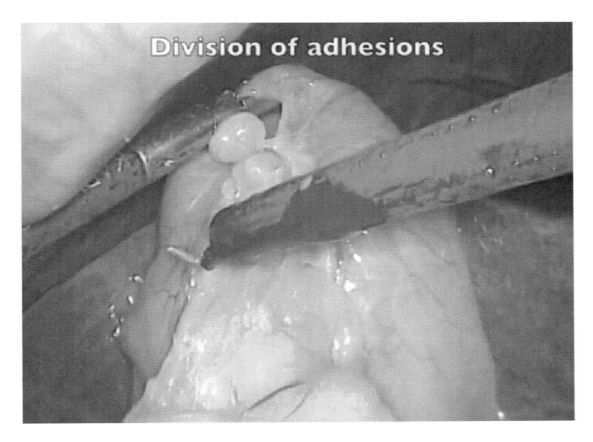

After this left hand forceps should grasp the Hartmann's pouch and it should be retracted laterally.

Now with retraction of fundus upwards, Hartmann's laterally and duodenum displaced medially the peritoneal fold of cystic duct and cystic artery is placed on stretch.

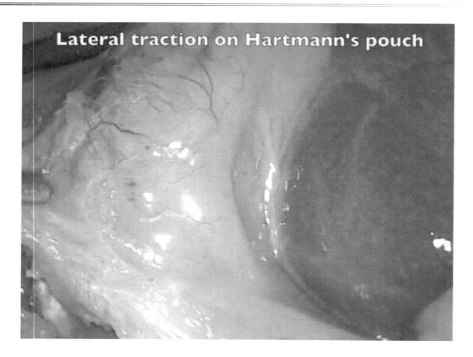

In laparoscopic surgery the left hand is vitally important as it alters the degree and direction of traction and it feeds tissue to the right hand for dissection, coagulation etc.

## STEP 3:

With the left hand lifting Hartmann's pouch upwards and laterally, the posterior aspect of Hartmann's pouch is displayed. Dissection commences in the safest area by division of peritoneal fold between the Hartmann's pouch and liver. With the help of curved dissectors or hooked dissector the posterior junction of gallbladder and cystic duct is clearly defined in this manner by dissecting deeper and medially a posterior window is created and the commencement of the cystic duct till the liver can be seen through this window.

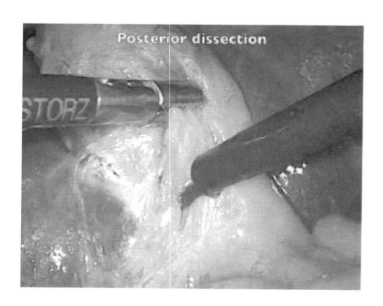

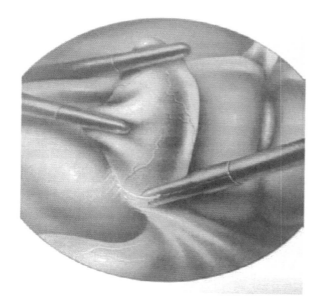

Once the window and clearance of gall bladder cystic duct junction and lateral aspect of the duct is completed posteriorly, anterior dissection is commenced.

Traction on Hartman's pouch is now altered to pull it downwards and laterally exposing the anterior peritoneal fold of calots. The cystic artery is identified at this stage and dissected from the cystic duct. Dissection of cystic duct should be carried with firm lateral traction on Hartman's pouch. Dissection of cystic duct should be stopped about 1 cm from common bile duct.

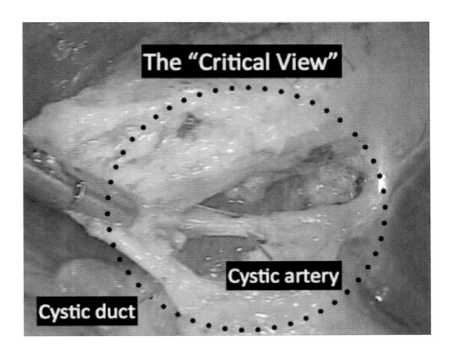

The more the adhesions or if the anatomy is not clearly defined the dissection should move further up to the neck of gall bladder so that entire circumference of the gall bladder is dissected at the neck before dissecting the cystic duct. It should be kept in mind that dissection is always in the direction from the gall bladder towards the common bile duct.

Once the cystic duct is adequately dissected and skeletonised laparoscopic cholangiography can be carried out if indicated. Then two medium sized clips are applied on the body of the artery and the third clip on the artery on the side of the gall bladder. An abnormally wide cystic artery should arise suspicion of a "humped" right hepatic artery with a short cystic artery which signifies the importance to dissect the cystic artery flush with the gall bladder.

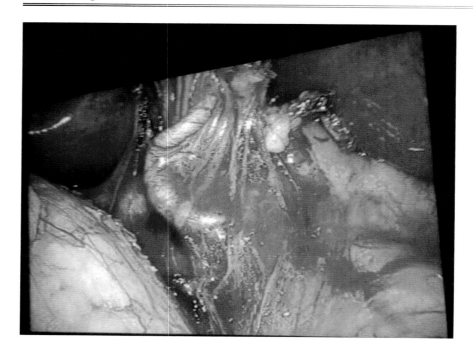
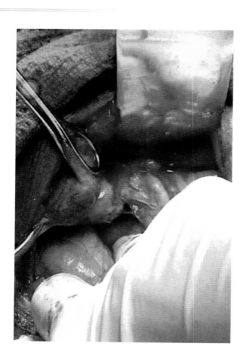

MOYNIHAN'S CATERPILLAR HUMP

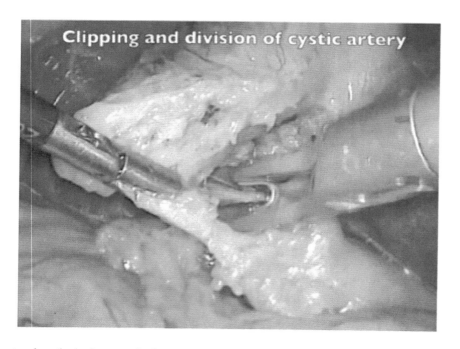

After the artery is divided the medial and lateral peritoneal fold extending upto the liver on either side of neck are divided so that the gall bladder-duct junction is fully mobilized to give elephant head appearance. Cystic duct should not be clipped till the elephant head is clearly demonstrated. Usually the reusable clip applicators with smaller medium sized clip LT300 is used to occlude the artery and coming to cystic duct medium clip is used for cystic duct upto 3 mm in diameter. For 3 to 5 mm sized cystic duct medium to large size clip is used, and for cystic duct over 5 mm ligature is done. The clip should be applied only after dissection of the entire circumference of cystic duct and artery. The size of various structures can be determined by comparing with known size of various instruments. The traction on hartmann's pouch by left hand should be given laterally and it is very important so that the cystic duct is at right angle to hepatic duct and common bile duct junction. The failure of lateral traction during cystic duct dissection or clipping is an important cause of common bile duct Injury.

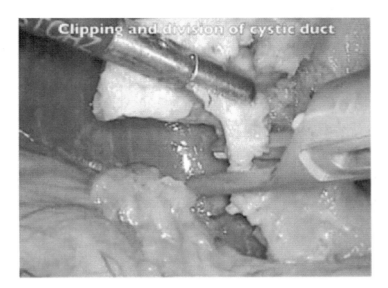
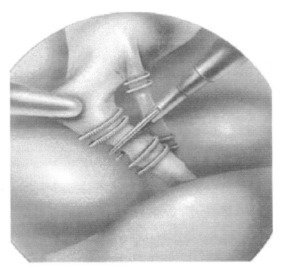

The clip should be applied at right angles to the structure to be occluded which is fed into the clip by left angled traction to ensure that the full circumference of duct/artery is within the clip. The position of common bile duct should be visualized before the occlusion. The lateral occlusion of left hand should be reduced just before clip occlusion or ligature of cystic duct to ensure that common bile dut is not entered into the clip or ligature. Atleast 0.5 cm cystic duct should be left medial to site of occlusion. Two clips on the body side and one at the neck of gall bladder should be applied and the duct is divided close to the one on specimen side. After dividing cystic duct and artery the stumps of both these structures should be carefully examined.

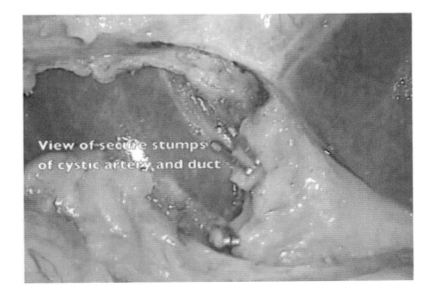

**STEP 4:**

After this the direction of traction on the gall bladder should be changed in such a way that the peritoneal folds are made taut. The gall bladder is gradually dissected from the gall bladder fossa starting from the neck and working towards the fundus. The traction direction and the degree of traction should be altered to keep the area under dissection on the stretch permitting smooth dissection of gall bladder. Sometimes we may enter the deeper plane into the liver tissue while dissecting gall bladder or conversely the gall bladder wall may be nicked. If opened the gall bladder wall around the rent should be held with a grasping forceps and a loop ligature or clipped around the tear.

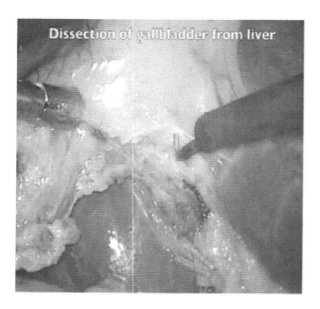
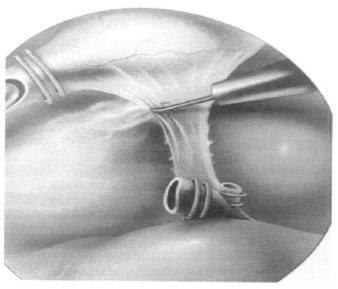

When there is goss fibrosis or adhesions at the neck of gall bladder and the integrity of common bile duct is compromised "fundus first" dissection should be done.

And if there is no plane of dissection between contracted Gall Bladder and the liver bed it is wise to excise the gall bladder leaving a small part of the wall stuck to the liver bed behind after sucking the bile and carefully collecting all spilled stones. Then the mucosa of the gall bladder will adherent to the liver is carefully diathermised.

Once hemostasis is secured abdomen is irrigated and sucked clean. The tilt and head high position of the patient is reversed. Then the abdomen is carefully examined for any fluid collection, pelvis and subdiaphragmatic areas.

The gall bladder neck is drawn into 11 mm trocar and gradually extracted from the abdominal cavity with the 11 mm trocar. After extraction, the umbilical site is temporarily occluded with the assistant's gloved finger so as to maintain the pneumoperitoneum. The middle and lateral ports are removed as the videoscope inspects for any bleeding at these sites. The videoscope is removed and the pneumoperitoneum is evacuated so as to lessen postoperative discomfort.

## Drainage

The situation where drainage procedure is appropriate is

1. Significant bleeding during the operation.

2. Significant bile leakage

3. Severe infection in acute cholecystitis.

When drainage is indicated the passive drainage system is recommended.

## Closure

The operative sites are infiltrated with a long acting local anesthetic (bupivacaine) and the fascia at the 10 mm port sites is resutured with one or two absorbable sutures. The skin is approximated with absorbable subcutaneous sutures. Adhesive skin strips and a dry sterile dressing are applied.

# 6

# Laparoscopic Surgery for Large Bowel

Laparoscopic large bowel surgery has not developed at the same rate as other procedures due to the need for advanced laproscopic surgical skills, difficult instruments and concern about port site recurrences in malignancies. Controversy exists as to whether colonic cancer surgeries should be carried out entirely laparoscopically as insufficient tumour clearance and difficulty in identifying ureter and duodenum exists. In addition, a small laparotomy has to be carried out to remove the excised tissues. Triangulation of the trocars and adequate creation of working space with table adjustments and carbon dioxide are mandatory for careful surgery. But patients appear to have an early return of bowel activity and ileus appears to be less.

## Right Hemicolectomy

- An umbilical port is introduced and a full assessment of the abdomen is made including inspection of liver for secondaries. The secondary trocars and cannulae are inserted as shown in the figure.

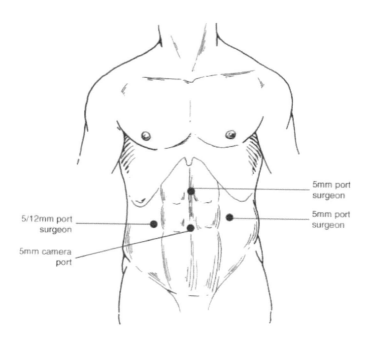

- Trendelenburg position is made.

- Caecum is grasped with a laproscopic Babcock forceps through working port in left iliac fossa and the clamp is lifted in the direction of spleen.

- Monopolar scissors is introduced through the working port in right iliac fossa and the fold of peritoneum at the base of caecum is divided.

- After mobilising the caecum by cutting the fascia of Toldt, the Babcock pulls the caecum and ascending colon medially.

- Then with the patient in reverse Trendelenburg position the hepatic flexure is mobilised.

- Congenital reflection of peritoneum in the right paracolic gutter is divided, including the hepatocolic ligament securing the hepatic flexure of colon.

- The right ureter is rarely seen and duodenum identified occasionally during laproscopic procedure.

- After mobilization of hepatic flexure, (care is taken to avoid the gall bladder as it comes to operative field) the specimen is ready to be delivered to the surface for resection.

- Small transverse muscle splitting incision is made in the right hypochondrium.

- After entering the peritoneal cavity the tumor and the colon are delivered with a combination of Babcock forceps attached to the bowel and a finger inserted into the incision. The pneumofflator should be switched off and the pneumoperitoneum released at this stage of procedure.

- When the specimen is at the surface a formal right hemicolectomy is performed.

- The right branch of middle colic artery, the ileocolic artery and the smaller mesentric vessels are ligated and divided.

- Ileo-colic anastomosis is done followed by closure of mesentery. The bowel is replaced back into abdomen and the wound closed.

- The pneumoperitoneum is re-established, irrigation of operation site is done and haemostasis is confirmed. Anastomosis can be done intra-corporeally using a stapling device though it still requires a small laparotomy to deliver the specimen.

- Post operatively patients take liquid diet from the first POD and can be discharged after 4–5 days. They can return to normal activities by 2 weeks.

## Left Colon and Rectum

Technically more demanding and time consuming when compared to right colonic procedures.

For all the left colonic and rectal procedures the port sites are as shown in the figure.

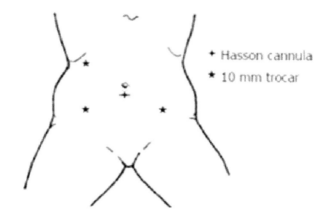

+ Hasson cannula
* 10 mm trocar

- Trendelenburg position.

- Surgeon on right side of patient.

- Camera assistant to left of surgeon.

- Monitor is placed at lower end on the left to face the surgeon.

## Mobilization of Left Colon

- Incision of congenital reflection of peritoneum in the left paracolic gutter and freeing of colon.

- Identification of left ureter.

- Ligation and division of inferior mesentric vessels.(stapling and division using automatic stapling device can also be done).

## Mobilization of Rectum

- Atraumatic clamp is placed across the upper rectum and pulled backwards towards the spleen, placing the peritoneum around the upper rectum under tension.

- Middle rectal vessels are identified and clipped.

- Rectum is mobilized under vision upto levator muscles.

- Ileo-rectal or ileo-anal anastomosis is done.

Mesenteric vessels can be stapled and divided and thus colon and rectum can be freed and removed without spillage of their contents. It is now possible to wash out rectal stumps like in open surgeries now that laproscopic atruamatic bowel clamps are available.

Depending on the site of lesion and indications, a colostomy or formal anastomosis can be done. This technique allows a variety of procedueres to be performed.

## Left hemicolectomy and sigmoid colectomy

Lloyd davies position with Trendelenburg tilt.

- Sigmoid colon is mobilised by traction and countertraction.

- Identification of ureter and rectosigmoid junction.

- Left colon is mobilised upto splenic flexure.

- The entire left colon should be mobilised and the colon so mobilised should go down easily into the pelvis.

- Small left iliac fossa muscle splitting incision.

- Division of mesenteric vessels.

- Laproscopic assisted resection done.

- Anastomosis is done on the abdominal wall.

- Intracorporeal anastomosis can also be done using a stapling device to divide the mesenteric vessels and bowel.

## Anterior resection of rectum-

- Rectum is mobilized fully.

- Inferior mesentric pedicle is ligated.

- Rectum divided above and below using a stapling device.

- Specimen is removed through a small incision and the anvil of the stapler is placed in the proximal bowel.

- Stapler is then introduced through the rectum and anastomosis is performed.

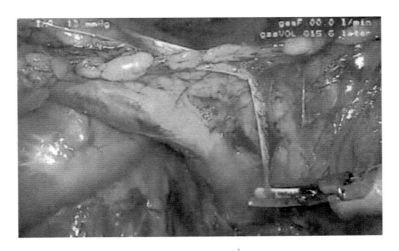

## Hartmann's Procedure

- Rectum and colon are mobilized.

- Bowel divided below the lesion using a stapling device.

- Incision made in the left iliac fossa.

- Specimen delivered and resected.

- Left iliac fossa colostomy is made.

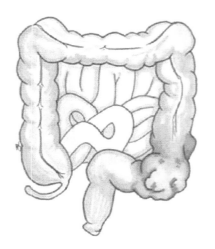 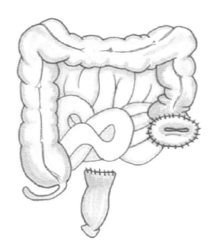

## Abdominoperineal Resection of Rectum

- In large lesions ureteric stents may help to identify the ureters.

- Urinary catheter is a must prior to surgery.

- Initial inspection of viscera including liver is made.

- Sigmoid colon is pulled to the right and the left para colic gutter adhesions are released.

- Left ureter and gonadal vessels are identified and preserved.

- Sigmoid colon is pulled to left and sigmoid mesentry is divided on the right

- Mesenteric vessels are identified.

- Inferior mesenteric vessels are tied and smaller vessels divided using harmonic shears or diathermy.

- Now telescope is shifted to the right iliac fossa and babcocks forceps through the left iliac fossa port holds the rectosigmoid junction exposing the rectum anteriorly and fascia of Waldeyer posteriorly. This avascular space is dissected down using diathermy.

- Lateral ligaments of rectum are divided the same way.

- Rectal dissection is mostly done from the right approach.

- Perineal resection is now started.

- Encircling stitch for anus.

- Skin is divided upto the ischiorectal fossa laterally and anococcygeal ligament is divided posteriorly.

- Presacral dissection is done anterior to coccyx.

- The levator and then the superficial transverse perineal muscles are divided.

- Then the anterior surface is divided at the posterior border of the deep transverse perineal muscle and the rectourethralis and puborectalis muscle are divided.

- Posteriorly the perineal surgeon tents the Waldeyers fascia which is then diathermised laproscopically from above.

- The fingers of the perineal surgeon can be seen laproscopically and the escape of pneumoperitoneum is prevented by a mop.

- The left colon is divided using a linear stapler.

- The proximal end is brought out through the left iliac fossa as an end colostomy.

- Specimen delivered through the perineum and the perinea! wound is drained.

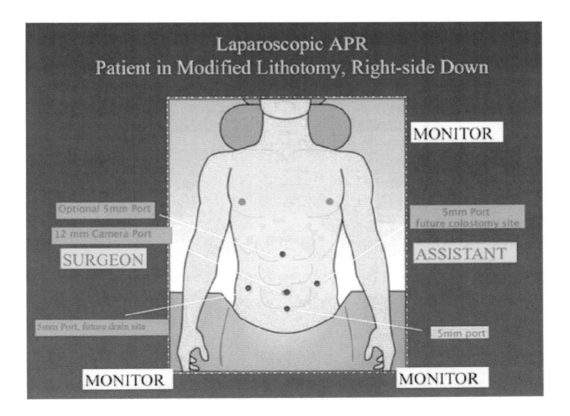

Laparoscopic APR
Patient in Modified Lithotomy, Right-side Down

## Sigmoid Colostomy

- Sigmoid colon is easily identifiable and is delivered out via a secondary port made in the left iliac fossa.

- Colostomy fixed to skin and is matured immediately or subsequently opened as warranted.

## Total Colectomy and Laproscopic Assisted Ileoanal Pouch

- Time consuming.

- Faster post operative recovery, with less post operative pain and chest complications.

- Used in ulcerative colitis and familial polyposis.

- Ileocolic junction is divided using an endostapler which closes off both the ileal and colic ends minimizing faecal spillage.

- The greater omentum is dissected away from the transverse colon.

- Sigmoid and left colon are mobilised.

- 5 cm vertical long incision is made supraumbilically and the terminal end is stapled with a long linear stapler using the limited incision to create J ileal pouch.

- Peranally submucosal dissection is done to raise the mucosa to perform mucosal protectomy.

- Rectum is divided and specimen is removed.

- J pouch is then brought down endoanally and secured with interrupted vicryl sutures to form ileoanal pouch.

- No ileostomy is required after ensuring the pouch is tension free.

- A drain is left to evacuate pelvis.

- Port sites and suprapubic incision sites are closed.

## Laproscopic Colonic Resection in Malignancies SAFE?

Attention to be given to

- Intro operative staging

- Palpation at open surgery is replaced by laproscopic USG probes

- No touch technique

- Studies have showed that no touch technique does not change the survival rates of potentially curative diseases. Hence early ligation of regional blood vessels is not required and not possible in laproscopic colectomy.

- Intro luminal spread

- It is sufficient to obtain 10 cm proximal and distal luminal margins and these can be achieved by laproscopic colectomy.

- Wide mesentric dissection

- Recent studies have showed no added survival advantage between radical hemicolectomy with segmental colectomy. This is important as laproscopic colonic resection is usually a segmental colectomy. Hence it is unlikely that a laproscopic colectomy will compromise patient survival.

However laproscopic colonic surgeries does has its limitations.

- Bowel obstruction – does not permit a formal bowel preperation and hence laproscopic colectomy is not feasible.

- Laproscopic anterior resection is limited by distal suture line. Tumors must be at least 14 to 15 cm from the anal verge to achieve adequate distal margin because the endo stapler is straight and stapled suture line can only be 10–12 cm from the anal verge.

## Port Site Recurrence

Local cellular trauma in both open and laproscopic surgery resulting from an incision or trocar contributes to a biologically favourable site for tumor implantation.

- Adherence of intravascular tumor cells to areas of local tissue trauma

- Local hyperthermia augmenting nutrient supply.

- Surgery induced depression of host immunity and release of tumor growth factors.

- The healing surgical incision that is a rich source of type IV collagenase that plays a major role in the invasion of tumor cells.

Several laproscopy specific factors may contribute to the tumor implantation in the lateral ports. There will be an increased concentration of exfoliated tumor cells at the port site which favours implantation. Free tumor cells could originate from

- divided serosa

- bowel lumen

- from divided lymphatic and blood vessels.

Either direct pressure on the tumor or from traction needed to expose it, application of grasping clamps could release tumor cells into inflamed peritoneal cavity or into veins or lymphatic vessels. Manipulation of tumor can cause exfoliation of liable tumor cells into colonic lumen. Local oxygen concentration also plays a part in tumor implantation.

How to prevent the complication of port site recurrence?

- Extraction of tumors through anal canal avoids some of the ways of port recurrence and is useful in sigmoidal and rectal resections

- Placement of specimen in a retrival bag may avoid incisional recurrences but does not affect intraperitoneal manipulation of the tumor.

## Rectopexy

- Magnification aids the careful dissection, avoiding nerve injury and placement of mesh. Surgeon stands on left of patient, camera assistant to his right. Assistant stands opposite to the surgeon on the right.

- 2 monitors are kept near the foot end of the patient on either side.

- Modified Lloyd davis position with urinary catheter.

- Subumbilical port and 3 working ports.

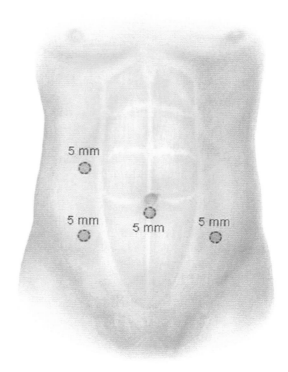

- Trendelenburg position.

- Babcock forceps inserted through the left port pulls up the rectosigmoid to the left and anteriorly. Another babcock forceps through the suprapubic port pulls the upper rectum anteriorly exposing the right side of rectum.

- Right ureter is identified and preserved.

- The peritoneum to the right of rectum is incised and dissection is carried out between the rectum anteriorly and fascia of Waldeyer posteriorly. The incision is carried down to the pelvic floor. Pelvic nerves are preserved.

- Similar procedure is carried out to expose the left side of rectum after identifying the left ureter. Posteriorly the earlier dissected space from the right side is met behind the rectum and is expanded to expose the pelvic floor.

- A curved dissector is used to hold the rectum anteriorly to pass the mesh behind. A 15 x 15 cm mesh is introduced to the presacral area and laid on the pelvic floor.

- Mesh is initially fixed to sacrum and presacral fascia using hernia staplers or silk sutures and then to the lateral rectal walls using at least 3 interrupted silk sutures.

- The peritoneum is then closed over the mesh using interrupted or continuous silk sutures. Post operatively bulk purgatives prevent the patient from straining at stools.

- Oral fluids and normal diet are started at the end of 24 hours. Discharged at 3–5 days.

# 7

# Laparoscopic Surgery for Peptic Ulcer

Laparoscopic surgery in peptic ulcer has many advantages over conventional surgery such as less pain, less complications, early return to work. The type of surgery may vary depending upon whether it is elective or emergency.

Vagotomy at elective surgery effectively reduces the acid production in many ways. The types of laproscopic vagotomies are-

1. Thoracoscopic truncal bilateral vagotomy-useful when there is recurrent anastomotic ulceration following earlier abdominal surgery.

2. Laproscopic truncal vagotomy with laproscopic stapled gastrojejeunostomy with lap-assisted or with laproscopic sutured GJ (intracorporeal) with pyloromyotomy or pyloroplasty with endoscopic balloon dilatation of pylorus.

3. Laparoscopic posterior truncal vagotomy and anterior seromyotomy.

4. Laparoscopic anterior and posterior highly selective vagotomy.

5. Laparoscopic posterior truncal vagotomy and anterior highly selective vagotomy-Useful in GOO along with acid output.

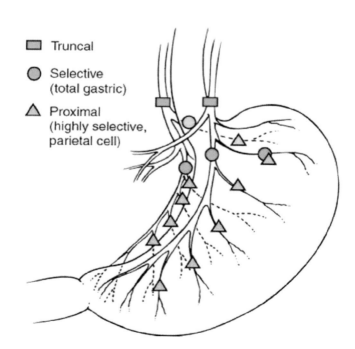

## 1. Thoracoscopic Truncal Bilateral Vagotomy

Useful when there is recurrent anastomotic ulceration following earlier abdominal surgery.

## 2. Bilateral Truncal Anterior and Posterior Vagotomy Followed by Drainage

**Procedures**

General anaesthesia

- o Modified Lloyd davis position with head end up.

- o Surgeon stands in between the legs, assistant to left of patient and camera assistant to right of patient.

- o Monitors above the shoulder of patient.

- o Umbilical 10 mm port, left (10 mm) and right (5 mm) midclavicular line, epigastrium 5 mm, left border of rectus midway between the umbilicus and xiphoid 10 mm.

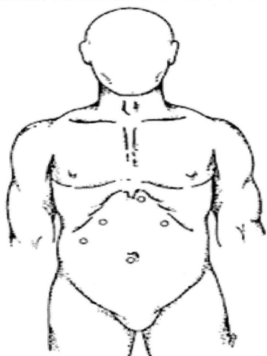

Angled 30 degree scope is more useful than 0 degree scope to visualise the lower end of oesophagus and the vagi.

- o Oesophagus identified by passing a bougie or via illuminating endoscope. Left lobe of liver retracted by passing a retractor through epigastric port. OG junction is grasped and pulled to the left and kept under traction.

o Gastrohepatic ligament is opened and peritoneum over the right crus of diaphragm is divided. Oesophagus skeletonised and pulled to left.

o Identification of posterior vagus as a white cord between the right crus and oesophagus. Clipping of posterior vagus at 2 places and a piece is removed for histology.

o Peritoneum over anterior surface of oesophagus is divivded. Anterior vagus is identified. It is embedded in the wall. Division of anterior vagus in the same way.

o 4–5 cm of oesophagus is skeletonised to divide all the branches of vagus given off higher up.

Drainage is achieved by stapled GJ

o Identification of jejunum to be anastomosed.

o Jejunum is brought forward through ante or retro colic routes and held together with the surface of stomach with two Babcock forceps.

o Using a L diathermy hook a small opening is made in the jejunum and stomach.

o Using Endo GIA with one jaw inside stomach and another inside jejunum, it is fired and anastomosis created.

o Jaws removed and hemostasis is confirmed.

o Opening crested with the diathermy hook is closed with 2–0 vicryl intracorporeal sutures. No drain is needed

o Port sites closed.

## Modifications

### A. ASSISTED GJ

• Cost effective method.

• Endo GIA used in the original procedure is expensive.

• After laproscopic bilateral truncal vagotomy, the sites of anastomosis on the stomach and jejunum are chosen and grasped.

• This site is apposed to the anterior abdominal wall by the shortest route.

• 4–5 cm incision is made at the corresponding anterior abdominal wall and $CO_2$ flow stopped.

• Stomach and jejunum are delivered extraperitoneally outside anterior abdominal wall.

- 4 layered anastomosis is done and is pushed back inside.(time is important as the tissues delivered out tends to swell up due to impeded venous return, hence it should be done quickly).

- Incision closed and abdomen reinflated.

- Haemostasis confirmed.

- Port sites closed.

## B. SUTURED GJ

- Cost effective method.

- Endo GIA used in the original procedure is expensive.

- After laproscopic bilateral truncal vagotomy, the GJ is carried out in 4 layers of vicryl sutures using intrcorporeal suturing technique.

- Time consuming method.

## C. PYLOROMYOTOMY

- Done after laproscopic bilateral truncal vagotomy.

- Laproscopic pyloromyotomy is done.

- Can use electrocautery or laser (can control depth).

## D. ENDOSCOPIC BALLOON DILATATION

- 54 to 60 Fr calibre balloon dilatation catheter passed via endoscope to pylorus and is dilated.

- Can be done under laproscopic control or independently.

## 3. Laparoscopic Posterior Truncal Vagotomy and Anterior Highly Selective Vagotomy

o Anterior vagal trunk is identified and preserved.

o Serosa over the anterior vagus is divided and its branches to the fundus and antrum are identified. The nerve to antrum and pylorus (crow's feet) is preserved.

o Dissection starts from here proceeding upwards.

o Each branch is dissected for a length of 1 cm and divided between two clips. No need for drainage procedure.

## 4. Laparoscopic Truncal Vagotomy and Anterior Seromyotomy

- o Based on the principal that division of the seromuscular layer along the lesser curvature divides the smaller branches.

- o Seromyotmoy is begun 6 cm from the pylorus at 1.5 cm from the lesser curvature on the anterior surface of the stomach using hook diathermy.

- o Myotomy proceeds from below upwards and extends across the OG junction onto the posterior aspect of cardia.

- o Seromyotomy is closed with continuous vicryl sutures. Posterior truncal vagotomy is combined with this procedure. No drainage procedure is needed.

- o Mucosal integrity is confirmed by intragastric instillation of methylene blue dye.

## 5. Anterior and Posterior Highly Selective Vagotomy

- o Time consuming

- o Not superior to other methods.

## Laparoscopy in Duodenal Ulcer Perforation

- • Modified lithotomyposition.

- • GA

- • Subumbilical 10 mm port, 2 ports in the left and right midclavicular line midway between the subcostal margin and umbilicus.

- • Suctioning and irrigation of the soiled peritoneal cavity.

Any of the following procedures may be done.

1. Small and moderate perforations require intracorporeal suturing of the perforation with vicryl sutures with a piece of omentum over it. Usually 2 sutures are enough.

2. Gastroscope introduced per operatively is used to pass a grasping forceps via the defect which grabs the omentum and pulls it up. The sutures then reinforce the closure.

3. Large perforations > 1 cm in the anterior wall of stomach can be converted to a gastrostomy by passing a Foley's catheter. Alternatively they can be closed with interrupted vicryl sutures and a patch of omentum. Biopsy from the edges is mandatory.

4. Gelatin sponge plug and fibrin glue have been used and does not require suturing.

# Laparoscopic Gastrostomy

- Used for feeding purpose as a temporary measure.

- Used in patients with head injuries who require prolonged ventilation and have intact gag reflux.

- Also used in pre-operative cases of carcinoma oesophagus to improve nutritional status. Supraumbilical 10 mm port.

- Additional subxiphoid port if left lobe of liver is enlarged to retract it.

- Another port to the left of midline usually midway between the xiphoid and the umbilicus. Using this port the anterior wall of stomach is picked up and exteriorised.

- A Malecot catheter is inserted inside the stomach lumen.

- It is fixed to the external skin after apposing the stomach wall to the anterior abdominal wall.

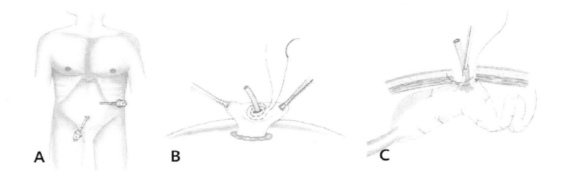

# Laparoscopic Gastrectomy

Time consuming procedure.

Requires skill in intracorporeal techniques of tying and suturing.

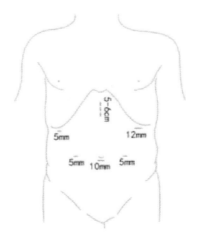

- Modified Llyod davis position.

- Surgeon standing between the legs of the patient. Head end of patient is tilted up.

- Greater omentum is detached along its entire length with transverse colon using harmonic shears.

- Stomach is pulled down to the left and lesser omentum is divided. Division of right gatric and right gastroepiploic arteries intracorporeally.

- Stomach is pulled up and the posterior aspect of the first part of duodenum is divided. Stomach is pulled up to the left and left gastric artery is ligated.

- Dissection of lesser omentum from the common hepatic duct and common bile duct. Stomach is divided with harmonic shears to achieve good cut ends with no bleeding. GJ using endostaplers (green) intraabdominally or laproscopic assisted GJ.

## Laparoscopic Jejunostomy

- Indicated for feeding malnourished patient with functioning gut where gastrostomy is not possible.

- In patients with upper git malignancies or in patients with neurological problem with severe head injury with prolonged coma.

- Can be done under GA or LA depending on general condition of patient. Modified lithotomy position.

- Surgeon stands between the legs of the patient.

- Cameraman on the right, scrub nurse on the left of the patient. TV monitor on each shoulder of patient.

- Subumbilical entry.

- Position changed to reverse Trendelenburg position.

- Trocars inserted on each semilunaris midway between umbilicus and xiphoid process, the left being 10 mm trocar and the right being 5 mm trocar.

- Omentum identified and pushed to expose the transverse colon. Jejunum traced upto DJ flexure.

- With the left trocar the jejunum is grasped after choosing appropriate site. $CO_2$ let out and jejunum is exteriorised.

- Using a diathermy a small incision made in the jejunum.

- A Foley's catheter is introduced (16F) into the jejunal lumen distally and bulb is inflated with 2 ml distilled water.

- Interrupted vicryl sutures appose the seromuscular layer of jejunum to the subcutaneous layer.

- Ports removed and closed.

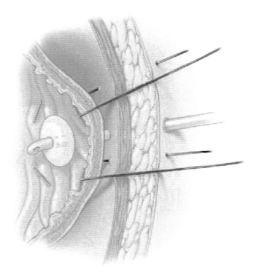

Feeding started after 24 hours.

Modifications include

1. Specialised T fasteners to appose the jejunum to anterior abdominal wall.

2. Using Ryle's tube instead of Foley's catheter using Witzel technique of burying it in seromuscular plane.

# 8

# Laparoscopic Ventral Hernia Repair

Almost all ventral hernias are amenable to laparoscopic repair.

**HISTORY:** The laparoscopic repair of ventral hernias was reported in early 1990s.

**PRINCIPLE:** The repair is based on the principle of the RIVES — STOPPA OPEN RETRORECTUS TENSION FREE MESH REPAIR. But here in laparoscopic approach, the mesh is placed in the intraabdominal cavity rather than in the retrorectus plane.

## Contraindications

1. Very large hernias with redundant skin folds.

2. Redundant abdominal wall requiring abdominoplasty.

3. Patients requesting improved cosmesis.

4. Patients having undergone multiple surgeries with dense intraperitoneal adhesions.

## Advantage

1. Patients with Swiss Cheese defects are greatly benefited by this approach as all defects can be clearly visualized and adequately covered.

2. Patients with large defects are also found to be benefited from this approach.

## Position

- The patient is placed in supine positon with arms tucked at the sides usually to allow the surgeon to move about.

- The position of the surgeon, first assistant and the monitor vary according to the site of the defect. The operating surgeon, the defect and the monitor should be in a straight line.

Operation theatre lay out for Upper midline hernias

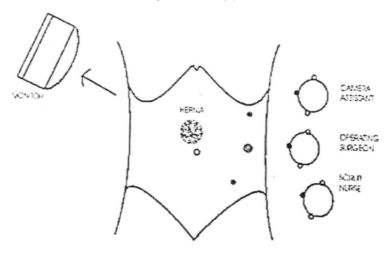

Operation theatre lay out for Lower midline hernias

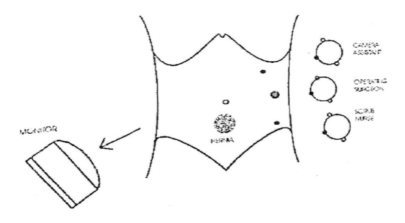

Operation theatre lay out for left flank hernias

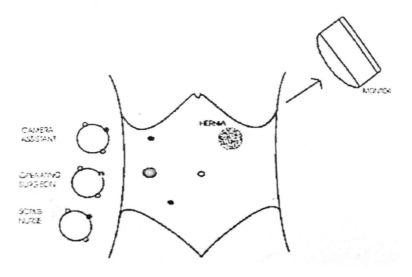

- The first trocar is placed at least 10 cm away from the edge of the hernia defect, preferably in the left hypochondrium, where it is least likely to traumatize the stomach.

- Three relatively safe areas for access include

    - The subxiphoid midline where the left lateral lobe of liver protects other organs

    - And each subcostal space at the anterior axillary line, where the presence of adhesions are rare.

    - The remaining two trocars are placed in line with the first trocar under vision.

Optimal position of ports

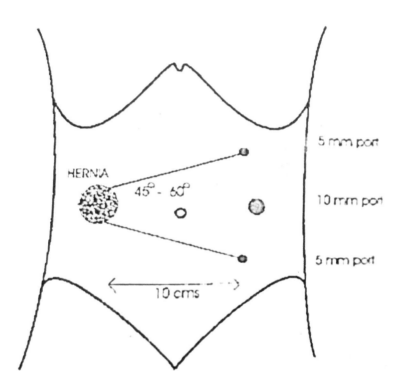

- The intertrocar distance is kept to a miniumum of 5 cm.

- A 30 degree telescope is used.

- The repair begins by reducing the contents of the sac. This is facilitated by external pressure applied manually over the defect.

- Once all contents are reducd and adhesions lysed, the edges get clearly defined.

- The lysis of adhesions is the most difficult and dangerous portion of this operation.

- An appropriate sized mesh is placed over the defect.

- The size of the mesh is measured as accurately as possible. The abdomen must be deflated while measuring the size to minimize the difference between the skin and peritoneum. In the presence of multiple defects, the maximum distance between all defects is measured and one mesh is used to cover all defects.

- The reason for placing the trocar at a distance of 10 cm from the defect is to allow for wide mesh coverage.

- The mesh is fixed to the margins of the defect using tackers.

- The omentum may be spread optionally over the bowel as a barrier between it and the mesh.

- Hemostasis is ensured.

- Instruments are removed and wound is closed.

## Complications

1. Seroma formation in the redundant sac: Pressure dressings should be used for 10–14 days.

2. Recurrence:

   – Strict adherence to surgical principles should be done.

   – Mesh should overlap 3 cm all around the fascial defect.

   – Excessive tension should not be present.

   – There should be no space between the mesh and the abdominal wall.

3. Bowel adhesions and fistula formation.

4. Wound infection.

# 9

# Laparoscopic Repair of Inguinal Hernia

What else could be an achievement than to have found a way to treat the most common general surgical problem by means of laparoscopy with less complications and more benefits!! Learning this novel technique might in future become a very basic requirement for any surgeon. Thorough knowledge and adequate training will thus help any surgeon to face this challenge and this chapter is focused to help you in a probably small way to help you do the same!

## Topics

- Laparoscopic Anatomy of the inguinal region

- Trans Abdominal PrePeritoneal Repair (TAPP)

- Totally Extra Peritoneal (TEP) mesh repair

- Complications of laparoscopic hernia repair

## Laparoscopic Anatomy of the Inguinal Region

A safe and successful outcome of any surgery is greatly dependent on a clear understanding of the anatomy of the area being operated. Learning the laparoscopic anatomy of the inguinal region is different and requires a radical shift in paradigm as we are used to learning anatomy from the outside! When the camera enters the abdomen there are important landmarks to look for.

i) **Median umbilical ligament:** This is a fold of peritoneum that stretches from the umbilicus to the dome of the bladder and is actually a remnant of the urachus. This serves as a guide for midline.

ii) **Medial umbilical ligament:** This stretches lateral to the previous ligament from the umbilicus to inguinal ligament and contains the obliterated umbilical artery. The laparoscopic importance of this structure is that it forms the lateral border of the bladder and is taken as the medial limit of incision in TAPP repair.

iii) **Lateral umbilical ligament:** This forms the medial aspect of the deep inguinal ring and encloses in itself the inferior epigastric artery. This thus serves as the landmark to differentiate direct and indirect inguinal hernia.

iv) **Deep inguinal ring:** This is an aperture seen just lateral to inferior epigastric artery. It transmits many structures namely Vas deferens and its artery, cord structures including the testicular artery and vein, genital branch of the genitofemoral nerve.

v) A transverse ligament like structure, the **Iliopubic tract** is seen extending from the pubic region to the anterior superior iliac spine and is the inner counterpart of the inguinal ligament. Any structures below the iliopubic tract should not be carelessly handled, dissected or tacked.

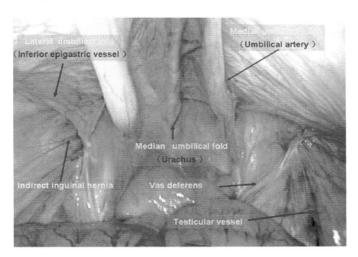

**Myopectineal orifice of Fruchaud** is the primary area of weakness through which most ofthe inguinal hernias occur. The boundaries of this orifice are

- Superior: Conjoint tendon.

- Medial: Lateral border of rectus abdominis.

- Lateral: Iliopsoas muscle.

- Inferior: Pecten pubis.

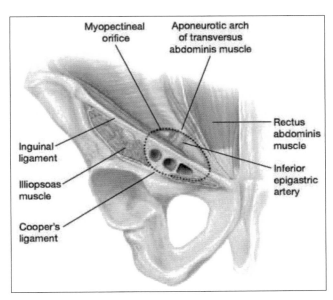

Knowledge about the **Preperitoneal Space** is very important for laparoscopic hernia repairs as this is the space where the mesh will be placed. The true preperitoneal space lies between the anterior and posterior layer of the transversalis fascia and is a potential space that needs to be dissected, developed and expanded to place a mesh inside it. The posterior layer of the transversalis fascia is filmsy and adherent to the peritoneum. This space is filled by a variable amount of connective tissue marked by avascular glistening web like white loose alveolar tissue.

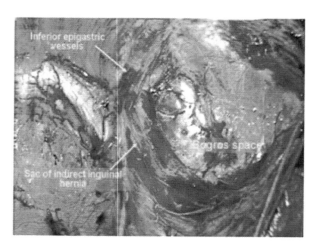 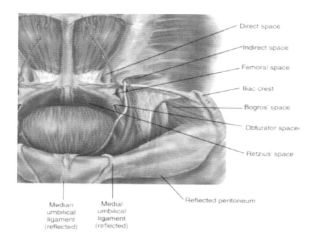

The **Retropubic space of Retzius** contains the accessory Obturator artery, abberant Obturator and retropubic veins, which when injured can cause troublesome hemorrhage. This space lies between the transversalis fascia and prevesical fascia & urinary bladder. Inferiorly this space extends below the pubic symphisis pubis upto the pelvic diaphragm. It is laterally limited by the Inferior epigastric artery.

The **space of Bogros** lies lateral to the inferior epigastric artery, upto the anterior superior iliac spine. Medially it continues with the space of Retzius. Posteriorly it is limited by the endopelvic and retroperitoneal fascia covering the iliopsoas.

# Blood Vessels of the Inguinopelvic Region

The external iliac artery and vein originate near the pelvic brim and course along the Psoas muscle to inguinal region. They give rise to inferior epigastric artery and vein just before entering the compartment below the iliopubic tract and inguinal ligament. The vas deferens crosses them from the deep inguinal ring from the lateral to medial aspect. The testicular vessels course beside these vessels laterally forming an angle with the vas in which the **External Iliac Vessels** lie. This is called the **Triangle Of Doom.**

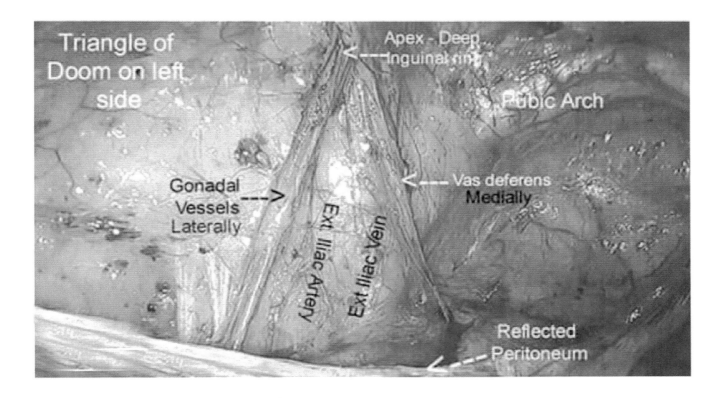

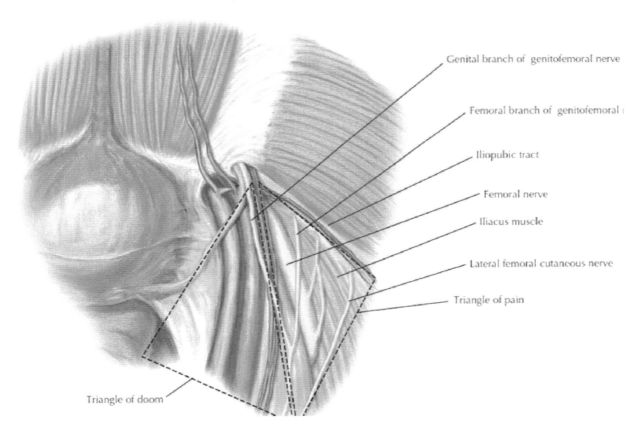

TRIANGLE OF DOOM

The testicular vessels arise from the abdominal aorta and travel along the Psoas to the internal inguinal ring.

The obturator vessels arise from the Internal iliac vessels and course along the obturator internus deep in the lateral wall of the pelvis. The **Accessory Obturator Vessels** especially the artery can arise from them and course along the Cooper's ligament vertically upwards to join the inferior epigastric arteries. These accessory obturator vessels can cause very troublesome bleeding since they are supplied by arteries at both ends. Hence the area on the cooper's ligament where they cross is called the **Corona Mortis.**

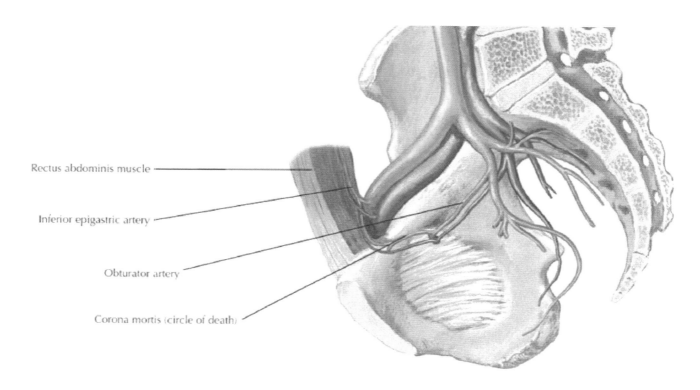

Rectus abdominis muscle

Inferior epigastric artery

Obturator artery

Corona mortis (circle of death)

CIRCLE OF DEATH

# Nerves of Inguinopelvic Region

i) **Genital branch of genito femoral nerve** pierces the iliopubic tract very near to the deep inguinalring.

ii) The**Femoral branch of genito femoral nerve** courses on the psoas and and enters the thigh along with it, below the iliopubic tract.

iii) The **lateral cutaneous nerve of thigh** enters the thigh below the iliopubic tract about 1–2 cm medial to anterior superior iliac spine. It is the lateral most nerve in the triangle of pain. Any injury to this nerve can cause severe paraesthesia in the anterolateral part of thigh.

iv) The **femoral nerve** is not seen during laproscopy but lies between the psoas and the iliacus. Any inadverdant injury to this nerve can cause sensorimotor loss and a crippling atrophy of the Quadriceps femoris.

v) Care must be taken not to injure the **Ilioinguinal and iliohypogastric nerves** while placing tackers.

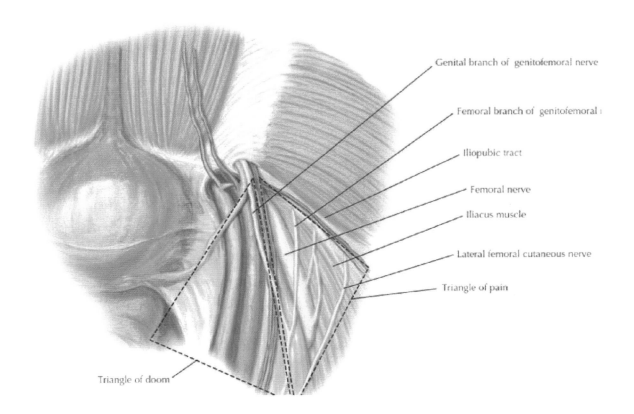

TRIANGLE OF PAIN

The **Triangle Of Pain** is formed by the iliopubic tract anterosuperiorly, testicular vessels medially and the reflected peritoneum. It contains the femoral, genitofemoral and lateral cutaneous nerves which when injured can cause severe pain.

# Transabdominal Preperitoneal (TAPP) Repair

## The Concept

This surgery involves entering the peritoneal cavity laparoscopically and then incising the peritoneum above the inguinal hernia defect and dissecting it off the abdominal wall along with the hernia sac. The mesh is then placed and fixed against the inguinopelvic region, and the peritoneal inscison is closed.

## Advantages

TAPP is easier to learn and has a shorter learning curve since all laparoscopic surgeons are familiar with accessing and operating in the intra peritoneal space.

## Indications

All kinds of inguinal hernia in patients who are fit for general anesthesia can be repaired by TAPP. However the universally accepted indications include:

1. Bilateral inguinal hernia

2. Irreducible or incarcerated inguinal hernia

3. Recurrent inguinal hernia after an anterior open repair

## Contraindications

1. Patient not fit for general anesthesia

2. Peritonitis or infection in peritoneal cavity

## Relative Contraindications

1. Prior pelvic surgery involving preperitoneal space like radical prostatectomy

2. Recurrent after previous TAPP

3. Previous surgery with extensive intra abdominal adhesions

4. Giant scrotal hernias

# Procedure

## Position of the Patient and Surgeon

- Supine position with both arms by the side.

- Reverse trendelenburg position of 15 to 20 degrees.

- The trolley with the monitor is placed at the foot end of the table/patient.

- The surgeon stands by the side of the patient on the side opposite to the hernia.

- The camera assistant stands on the side of the hernia.

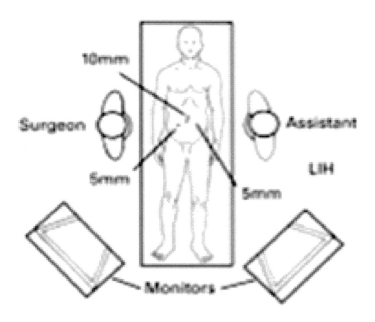

## Placement of Ports

- 10 mm supra/infra umbilical camera port.

- Two 5 mm working ports at the same level of camera just lateral to the rectus muscle. Care should be taken to not place these ports very laterally and far away because medial dissection will be difficult.

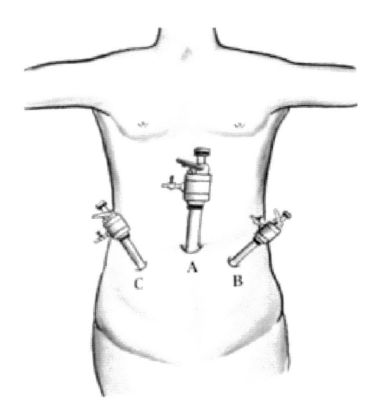

## Steps of the Procedure

1.  Creation of pneumoperitoneum

2.  Inspection of the inguinopelvic region for type of hernia, contents and anatomical landmarks

3.  Reduction of contents either by gentle manipulation with little pressure from the outside or usage of atraumatic graspers

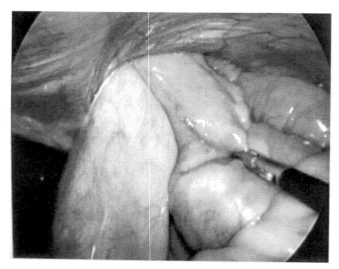

Reduction of contents

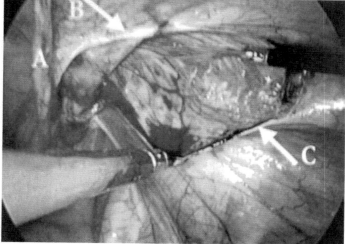

Peritoneal inscision above the defect

4.  Peritoneal incision:

    *   The Peritoneal incision is made from the ASIS to the medial umbilical ligament grasping the peritoneum using atraumatic graspers and using scissors to inscise the peritoneum

    *   The medial limit (medial umbilical ligament) should not be crossed for fear of injuring the urinary bladder

    *   The incision is made 4 to 5 cms above the superior margin of the hernia defect

    *   A curvilinear incision makes the lateral dissection easier

    *   The anterior lamina of the transversalis fascia covering the inferior epigastric artery and the transversalis muscle should not be incised

5.  Dissection:

    *   Loose areolar tissue seen is the plane to enter.

    *   The incised Peritoneum along with some fat is dissected off the anterior abdominal walllateral to the inferior epigastric artery.

- When the peritoneum is reflected laterally, the genito femoral nerve and the lateral cutaneous nerve of the thigh will be seen shining through the thin endopelvic fascia.

- Medial dissection is continued in the loose areolar tissue beyond the inferior epigastric vessels.

- The urinary bladder needs to be dissected off safely beyond the medial umbilical ligament. At this juncture the pubic rami and the shining white structure comes into view which is the Cooper's ligament. Thus the Coopers ligament is called "the light house" of the laparoscopic surgeon.

- The retropubic space of Retzius is also opened gently taking care not to injure any vessel (Accessory Obturator artery — Corona Mortis) or the Cooper's ligament.

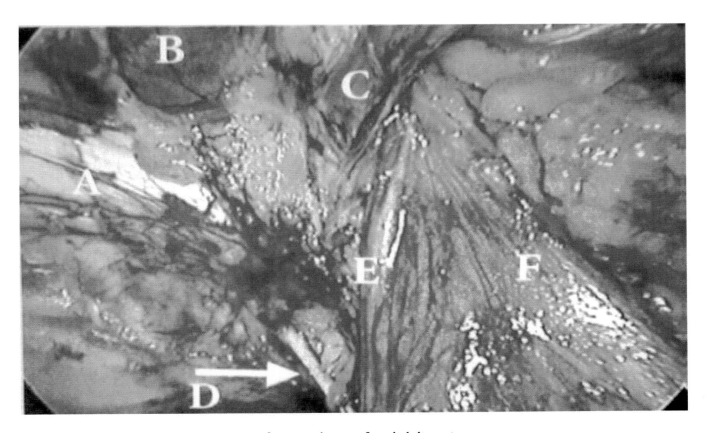

**Fig:** After completion of medial dissection.

- A) Right pubic rami
- B) Direct defect.
- C) Inferior epigastric vessels.
- D) Obturator vessls.
- E) Vas deferens
- F) Testicular vessels

- In direct hernia, medial dissection will essentially mean dissecting the sac of the abdominal and inguinal defect, taking care to dissect off the glistening white capsule of the transversalis fascia.

- The indirect sac is lateral to the cord. If it is small, it can be completely reduced whereas a complete sac cannot be completely reduced. In this situation, the indirect sac is dissected beyond the deep inguinal ring as much as possible and the sac is incised circumferentially & the distal sac is left off in situ in the scrotum. The peritoneal cut end of the sac is ligated with a loop of vicryl on a knot pusher or can be sutured.

- Completion of dissection is when medial dissection has crossed the midline by atleast 1 to 2 cms and the space of Retzius is completely open. The lateral limit of dissection is the anterior superior iliac spine.

6. Placement of mesh:

- A polypropelene or composite mesh of size 15 x 15 cms. It can be trimmed down to 12 x 15 cms and superolateral corner can be cut to fit it to the curve of lateral incision.

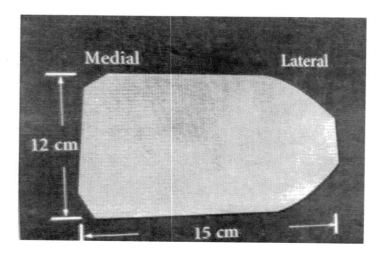

Size of mesh for a right side hernia.

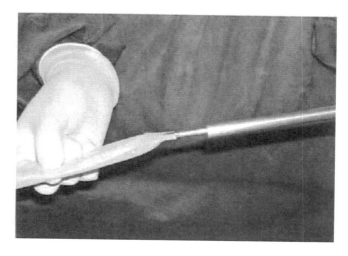

Reverse loading of the mesh

- The entire mesh can be either rolled like a cigar or folded on itself with anchoring vicryl sutures and reverse loaded onto a toothed grasper or needle holder and introduced into the peritoneal cavity.

- The mesh is placed about 1 cm medial to midline and then spread laterally.

- The lower 3–5 cms of mesh should be placed in the retropubic space and upper 2/3$^{rds}$ must lie flat against the anterior abdominal wall, so that it will not get rolled up or lifted up.

7. Fixation of the mesh:

- Fixation of the mesh is done either using tackers (absorbable or non-absorbable) or using sutures (2–0 prolene or PDS).

A minimum of two points or a maximum of four points is sufficient for fixation.

- Care must be taken to avoid injury to structures in the triangle of doom and triangle of pain, cord structures, inferior epigastric artery, accessory obturator artery and pubic vein.

- No tacker should be applied below the iliopubic tract.

8. Once the mesh is fixed, the peritoneum is sutured back using 2–0 vicryl so as to cover the entire mesh. Care should be taken not to leave any part of the mesh or tacker exposed.

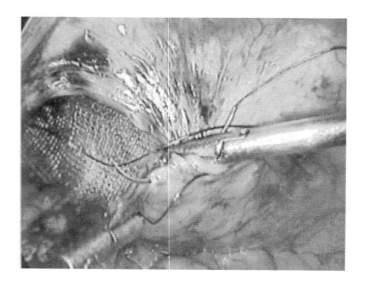 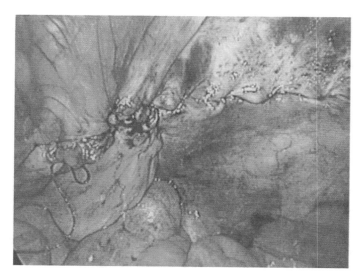

9. Desufflation and closure of abdomen.

# Total Extra Peritoneal (TEP) Repair

TEP potentially offers several advantages over TAPP repair including elimination of complications related to violation of the peritoneal layer and reduction of operative time especially for bilateral hernias.

The extraperitoneal approach is made possible by the fact that the peritoneum in the suprapubic region can be easily separated from the anterior abdominal wall and this space can be enlarged to help in dissection and placement of a mesh. Insufflation is usually done using a suprapubic Verress needle (Dulucq's technique).

## Port Placement

- 10 mm umbilical or infraumbilical camera port.

- First 5 mm working port contralateral to the side of hernia just near the midline.

- Second 5 mm working pararectus port on the ipsilateral side.

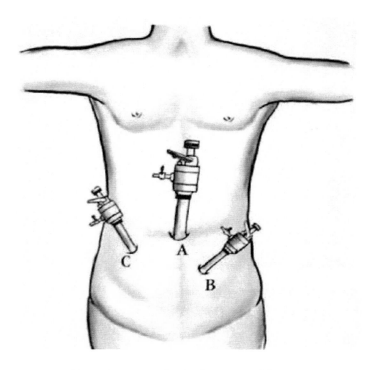

Port placement for Right inguinal hernia

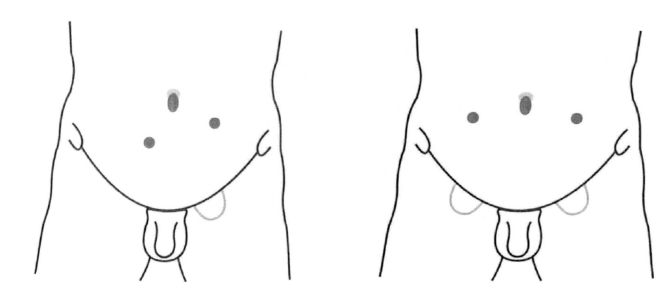

Port placement for Left hernia                 Port placement for bilateral hernia

# Procedure

- Insufflation is done at the level where cobweb like loose areolar tissue is encountered, moving the telescope forward and backward through the areolar tissue towards the symphisis pubis.care should be taken not to injure the inferior epigastric vessels or the nerves.

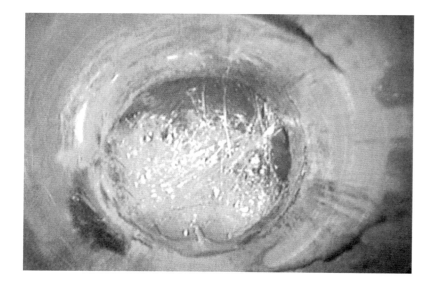

- Dissection is carried out medially upto the Cooper's ligament and laterally upto the visualization of the genitofemoral nerve.

- Placement and fixation of mesh is similar to TEPP repair.

- During desufflation, the mesh is held onto the anterior abdominal wall to avoid displacement or rolling up.

# Complications of Laparoscopic Inguinal Hernia Repair

## Introperative Complications

1. Bowel injury: Repair of the injury can be done laparoscopically or by open method and mesh fixation is postponed to a later period for fear of infection of the mesh.

2. Vascular injury: Timely decision to either control the bleed using harmonic scalpel, bipolar, clips or sutures or conversion to open procedure is crucial to avoid further complications.

3. Bladder injury: Bladder repair can be done laparoscopically and mesh fixation is postponed to a later period for fear of infection of the mesh.

## Postoperative Complications

1. Seroma formation.

2. Hematoma formation.

3. Mesh infection.

4. Inguinodynia due to injury to nerves.

5.  Injury to cord structures.

6.  Intestinal obstruction due to adhesion to exposed mesh or tacker.

7.  Port site hernia.

8.  Recurrence of hernia.

# 10

# Complications of Laparoscopy

There are two types of complications:

1. General

2. Procedure related.

## General

- Pneumoperitoneum related

- Access related

- Intra operative

- Electro surgical

- Post operative

## Pneumoperitoneum Related

- Gas embolism

- Cardiovascular complication

- Respiratory complication

- Shoulder pain

## Gas Embolism

- Incidence – .002 to 0.0016%

# Pathogenesis

During creation of pneumoperitoneum

Larger amount of $CO_2$

Enters the pulmonary circulation

V/Q mismatch

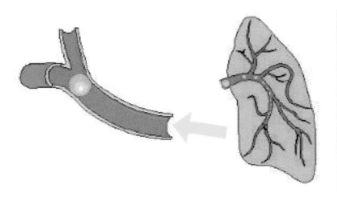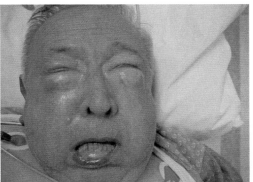

FEATURES OF GAS EMBOLISM

# Signs

- Tachycardia

- ↑CVP

- Hypotension

- Hypoxia

- Circulatory collapse

- Millwheel murmur

- ECG – Right Heart Strain

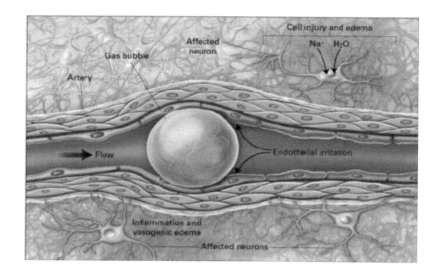

## Investigations

- Swan Ganz catheter confirm the aspiration of gas

- Precordial Doppler – Can detect 2 ml of gas

- Esophageal doppler – Can detect 0.5 ml of gas

- Capnometry – confirms the diagnosis

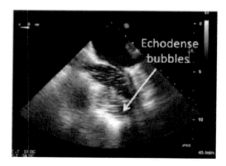
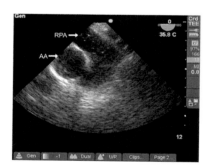

GAS EMBOLISM

## Treatment

- Slow insufflation and release pneumoperitoneum

- Steep head down and left lateral position (Durant position)

- $FiO_2\uparrow$ stop $N_2O$

- Hyperventilation

- CPCR

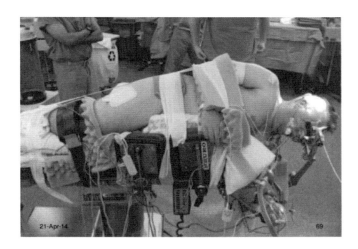

DURANT POSITION

## Cardiovascular Complications

The Carbondioxide absorbed in blood leads to hypercarbia and acidosis and thus it leads to myocardial irritability. This leads to:

- Arrhythmia

- Tachycardia

- Systemic hypertension

- Myocardial infarction

The increased intra abdominal pressure during pneumoperitoneum also leads to reduced venous return and Hypotension.

## Respiratory Complications

- Pneumomediastinum

- Pneumopericardium

- Pneumothorax

- Subcutaneous emphysema

Pneumothorax – Commonly occurs due to tear in the parietal pleura.

Eg; heller's myotomy and fundoplication

Pneumomediastinum – Through a defect in the Diaphragm or through oesophageal/aortic hiatus.

## Signs

1. $SpO_2$ fall

2. Cyanosis

3. Abnormal mobility of Hemidiaphragm

## Treatment

- Spontaneous resolution in 30 to 60 min ($CO_2$ soluble)

- Cessation of $N_2O$

- ↑$FiO_2$

- ↓Intra-abdominal pressure

- PEEP

- ICD if needed

## Shoulder Pain

Carbonic acid

| WATER + CABON DIOXIDE = CARBONIC ACID |

Peritoneal irritation

Diaphragmatic irritation (phrenic nerve)

Referred to shoulder

## Position Related Problems

- Over stretching of arm – brachial plexus injured.

- Lithotomic position – common peroneal and femoral nerve injured.

- Trendelenberg position reduces pulmonary reserve and causes GE reflux

- Prolonged lithotomy leads to lower extremity compartment syndrome.

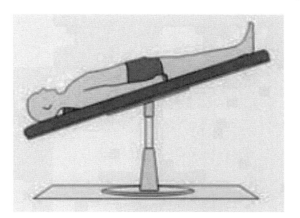 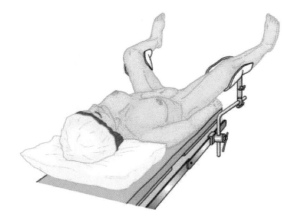

# Aspiration

- ↑Intra-abdominal Pressure leads to increased risk of regurgitation

- Functional changes are produced in LES

## Treatment

1. Usage of Preop antacid and $H_2$ antagonist

2. Usage of cuffed ET tube

3. Empty the stomach prior to pneumoperitoneum using Ryle's Tube aspiration.

## Git Injury

1. Abdominal wall:

   - extra peritoneal emphysema

   - Subcutaneous emphysema

   - Abdominal wall vessel injury

2. Intra abdominal:

   - Injury to Liver/spleen/bladder

   - Bowel Injury

   - Pneumoomentum

   - omental/mesentric vessel injury

3.  Retroperitoneal:

    – Injury to Aorta

    – Injury to IVC/Iliac vessels

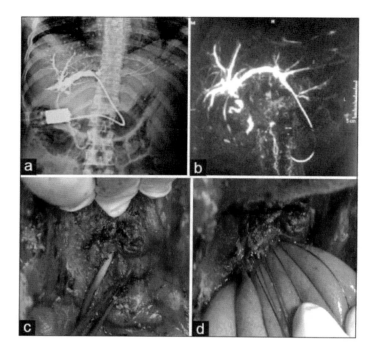

## Bowel Injury

- Most commonly small bowel>colon>duodenum>stomach

- Incidence – 0.06 to 0.4%; 5% mortality rate

- Most commonly during insertion of Veress needle and first trocar

- Prolonged manual ventilation → gastric distension

- Usually unrecognized, patient presents with post op peritonitis

## Should be Cautious in

- Previous midline scars

- Abdominal TB

- Disseminated Malignancy with peritoneal Carcinomatosis

**How to Avoid?**

While inserting Veress needle, Lift up the lower abdomen by using the left hand.

**Confirm by:**

1. Hissing test: After insertion of needle, the valve is closed and the abdominal wall is lifted. The valve is then opened. If properly positioned, due to negative intraa bdominal pressure, there will be a flow of air inside the abdomen and is heard as a hissing sound.

2. Drop test: A drop of saline is placed on the positioned needle and the abdominal wall is lifted, If the drop is sucked in, the needle tip is in the peritoneal cavity.

3. Free flow of 5 ml of saline into peritoneum.

**Management:**

• Early detection and repair

• Large perforation needs laparoscopic repair/laparotomy

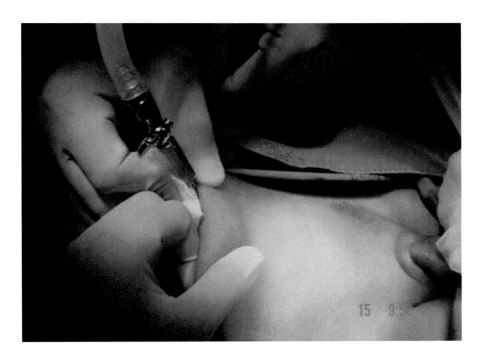

CORRECT METHOD OF INSERTION OF
VERESS NEEDLE

## Urinary Tract Injuries

• Most common in infra umbilical trocar insertion especially in appendix, hernia and gynaecologic surgeries.

• Usually in patients with full bladder and previous pelvic surgeries.

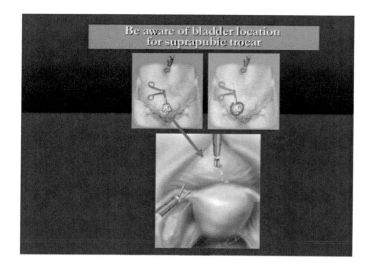

**When to suspect:**

- Saline test shows fluid resembling urine

- Hematuria and pneumaturia

- Confim by instillation of indigo carmine

## Treatment

- Foley's catheterization for 7 – 10 days

- Large rent should be repaired

## Prevention

- Preop catheterization for all cases

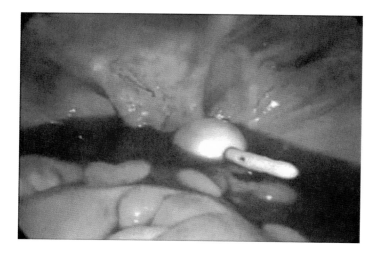

BLADDER INJURY

# Vascular Injuries

- During initiation of pneumoperitoneum

- Major cause of death, 15% mortality

- Due to improper insertion of Veress needle prior to insufflation/trocar inserted after insufflation

- Most common in thin people and children

- Most common vessel involved – right commom iliac and distal aorta

- Most common minor vessel injury is inferior epigastric vessels during hernia surgeries

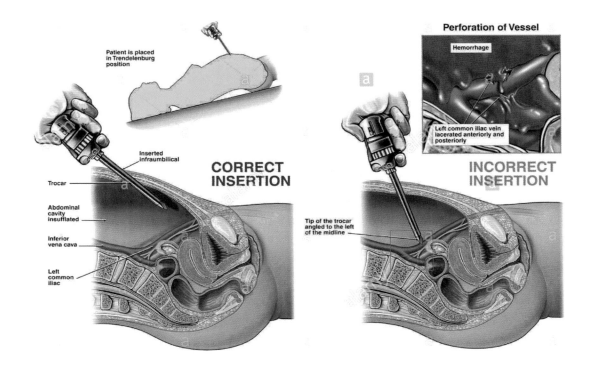

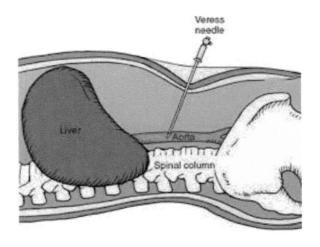

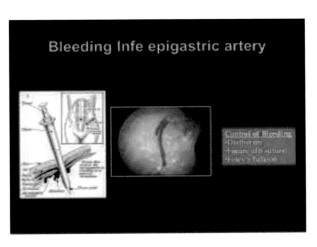

# Pitfall of Laparoscopy in Obesity

- Thick abdominal wall, more preperitoneal fat and fatty liver.

- Alteration in the length of the distance between Xiphisternum to umbilicus and from umbilicus to Pubis.

- Localisation of the tip of the needle is difficult.

- Lifting up of abdominal wall while inserting Veress needle, increases the distance the needle has to travel.

## How to overcome?

- Insertion Of Veress Needle at an angle of 90 degrees.

- Umbilical Entry/Open Technique (Optical/Direct Visual Entry).

- First trocar to be inserted 3 cm caudal the Left Subcostal plane in the Midclavicular line (Palmer's Point), because visceral-parietal adhesions are rarely found here.

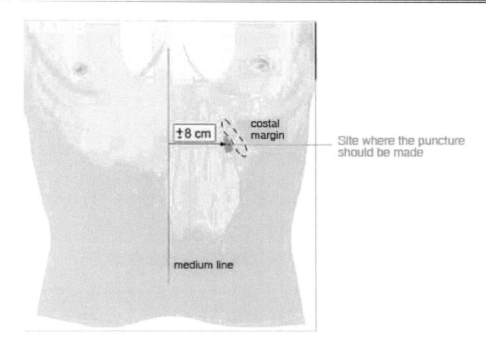

## Diathermy Injury

- Most common cause is insulation failure

- Direct coupling and capacitive coupling – Two modes of injuries

- Direct Coupling – When the electrosurgical device is in contact with a conductive instrument

- Capacitive Coupling – The electrosurgical instrument behaves as a capacitor and if the cauterizing current is activated before touching the target tissue, it may discharge through any tissue that is in contact with the device

- In 70% of individuals symptoms will be unrecognised

- Increased post op abdominal pain indicates injury

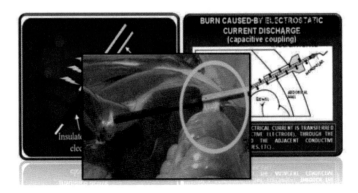

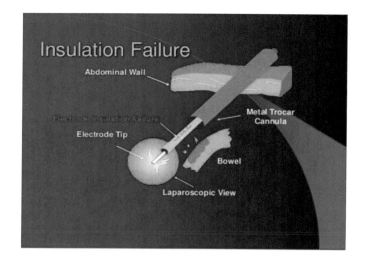

## Prevention of Diathermy Injuries

- Hand instruments should be examined periodically with lens for breech in the insulator.

- Prevent active electrode from touching other instruments.

- Use of bipolar coagulation/ultrasonic dissector.

## Treatment

- Superficial injury recognised during procedure – Prophylactic plication sutures.

- In full thickness injury – wide excision to include the area of coagulative necrosis.

- Injuries recognised during the postoperative period – should be treated as a usual perforation.

## Port Site Hernia

- Incidence 0.2 to 3%

- Due to inadequate fascial closure/infection

- Omentum and bowel are usually trapped at 3rd/5th POD

## Treatment

- Close the fascia with figure of 8 or simple suture.

## Prevention

- If port size > 5 mm stitch the fascia separately.

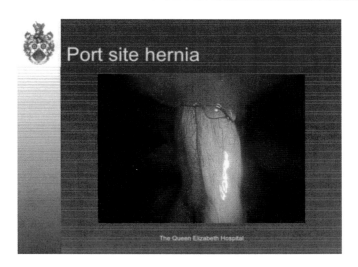

## Port Site Infection

- Most commonly due to retrieval of infected specimen.

## Prevention

- Use endobag.

- In case of a chronic sinus/granuloma not responding to usual antibiotics, Atypical Mycobacteria should be suspected.

- Regular self-wash of all the instruments.

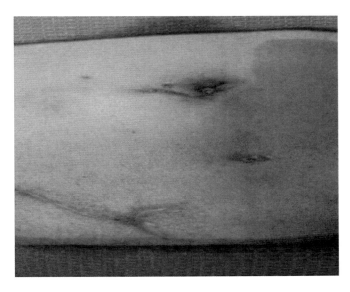

PORT SITE INFECTION

## DVT/Pulmonary Embolism

- Incidence – 0.1 to 0.9%

## Pathogenesis

Increased intraabdominal pressure

Compression of vein

Venous stasis in lower limb

DVT

## Treatment

- Early ambulation

- Subcutaneous heparin

- Anti embolism/compression stockings

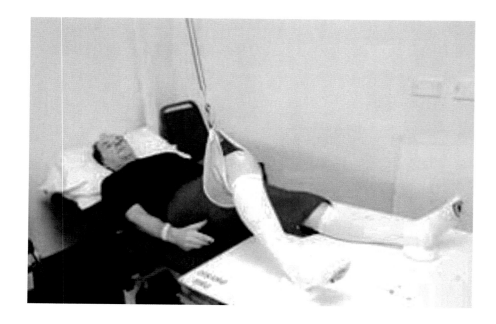

# Procedure Related Complications

| LAPAROSCOPIC PROCEDURE | COMPLICATION | PREVENTION |
|---|---|---|
| LAP APPENDICECTOMY | 1. Bleeding<br>2. **Stump appendicitis**<br>3. Wound infection | For stump appendicitis<br>1. Keep **stump size < 0.3 cm.**<br>2. Keep distance between 2 ligatures to < 0.5 cm. |
| LAP CHOLECYSTECTOMY | 1. **CBD injury**<br>2. Retained CBD stone<br>3. Bile leak<br>4. Bowel injury | Proper identification of<br>1. **Calots triangle** prior to clipping<br>2. Rouviers sulcus (above)<br>3. **Critical view of strasberg**<br>4. **Cystic node of lund (medial)** |
| LAP CBD EXPLORATION | **CBD Stricture (most common)** | 1. Avoid unnecessary use of diathermy<br>2. **Incision made vertical and wound close by horizontal suture** (3–0, 4–0 PDS) |
| LAP HERNIA | 1. **Hematoma and seroma (50 to 60 %)**<br>2. **Visceral injury**<br>3. **Vascular injury**<br>4. **Ileus and bowel obstruction**<br>5. **Urinary retention** | For seroma<br>1. Taking a stitch after reducing the sac at the most prominent part of hernia and suturing it to Coopers ligament to obliterate dead space. |
| LAP VENTRAL HERNIA | 1. **Seroma**<br>2. **Mesh migration**<br>3. **Incidental enterotomy** | 1. Interupted suture/binder<br>2. Trans abdominal fixation with additonal tackers |

# Laparoscopy During Pregnancy

1. It increases the risk of abortion or preterm labour.

2. Surgery should be planned during second trimester to minimize the risk of preterm labour and to have adequate working space.

3. Open method of pneumoperitoneum creation is preferred to avoid uterine injury.

4. Fetal monitoring with transvaginal Ultrasonography.

5. Maternal $PaCO_2$ should be maintained at normal levels.

6. Gasless laparoscopy/$N_2O$ may be considered.

## Patient Selection Aspects

1. Increased Intracranial tension and Glaucoma – Laparoscopy contraindicated.

2. Patients with Intraperitoneal, Peritoneojugular, VP shunts – contraindicated.

3. LV Dysfunction and CAD – Risk-Benefit ratio should be carefully analysed.

Made in the USA
Middletown, DE
28 February 2023

25875066R00077